BEAUTIFUL
BRITAIN

BEAUTIFUL BRITAIN

TAJ BOOKS

Published by TAJ BOOKS
27 Ferndown Gardens
Cobham
Surrey
KT11 2BH
United Kingdom
www.tajbooks.com

ISBN 1-84406-000-4

Printed and bound in China

Designed by bigmetalfish.com

CONTENTS

INTRODUCTION

INTRODUCTION

In prehistoric times the British Isles were joined to the Continent of Europe by a land bridge, but as the seas rose the islands became cut off from the mainland. Ever since then these islands have developed their own unique identity, ultimately developing a culture, and above all language, that has global significance.

Some of the earliest examples of the work of prehistoric man lie in Great Britain, including the most famous and mysterious of all monuments, Stonehenge, still magnificently situated in isolation on top of the Wiltshire hills. Nearby is the mysterious village of Avebury, entirely enclosed within a vast stone circle. In fact Britain is littered with prehistoric monoliths, stones, barrows, earthworks, and circles left from earlier times. Stone Age man has left only scattered remnants for archaeologists to discover but enough remain to show what great skills he possessed. Many such artefacts can be admired in local museums across the country as well as at the great institutions such as the British Museum in London.

Bronze Age and then Iron Age man developed increasingly sophisticated tools and, as life became more than a subsistence struggle, practised sophisticated farming methods; extended families lived in hill forts such a Maiden Castle in Dorset. Trade started in the earliest days and British sailors traded far and wide across the seas to the Mediterranean and beyond. With the rise of the Roman Empire it was only a matter of time before the Rome decided to take this rich territory for itself. Julius Caesar famously arrived in 55 and 54BC but returned to Gaul both times. In AD43 the Emperor Claudius sent four legions to conquer Britain. The Romans fought hard and ruthlessly with overwhelming military power, extending their influence to all but the fringes of the islands. In AD61 they met with great resistance from Queen Boudicca and her Icini tribe, but despite heroic endeavour the Romans prevailed. They built a backbone of roads linking their cities (often built on top of native Briton settlements) across the country all the way north to almost the borders of Scotland where they built Hadrian's Wall (started in AD12), and then later and further north, the Antonine Wall (c.AD140). Enough of the Wall remains to give a flavour of this furthermost outpost of Empire. The Romans stayed in Britain until AD410 when the empire collapsed, forcing their withdrawal. Roman villas and temples as well as much smaller artefacts are continuously found across all the parts of the country settled by the Romans.

When the Romans left central rule disappeared and the native Britons were left to fend for themselves against successive waves of invading Angles, Saxons, and Vikings tempted from the Continent by the rich pickings in Britain. The country was an ever-shifting matrix of small kingdoms, fiefdoms, and political alliances. But the English were just about uniting under their chosen Anglo-Saxon king when the Norman Duke William used his military might to enforce his rule after victory at the Battle of Hastings in 1066. He started the hugely unpopular Norman rule of England that has left an impressive legacy of castles and cathedrals across the country. One of the most famous of these is the Tower of London. Impressive today, it was an awesome symbol of the implacable might of the Normans to the subjugated Anglo-Saxons. The Normans codified and regulated their new lands and compiled the great Domesday Book, a detailed record of all their feudal holdings and all the taxes due to them. England became a unified country for the first time since the Romans left 600 years earlier. Once established in England, they moved to take control of Wales and Ireland taking all possible lands into their tight feudal fists.

Under the Norman kings was established a powerful aristocracy inextricably bound by feudal vows of loyalty and obedience; this, in turn, ruled an underclass of Anglo-Saxons. In time the power of the barons rebounded on the monarchy when King John was forced to sign the Magna Carta in June 1215 at Runnymede, conceding rights and privileges to his subjects and limitations on royal power.

After many years of border wars England and Wales were united by the Statute of Rhuddlan, proclaimed by Edward I in 1284. This set up colonial

INTRODUCTION

government institutions for the Principality of Wales. From then on the monarch's oldest son and successor was invested as the Prince of Wales with lands and privileges of his own.

In the fourteenth century England was engaged in the long on-off conflict against France known as the Hundred Years War, which actually lasted from 1337 until 1453. During this period the English Crown held and fought for great tracts of land in France and laid claim to the title of King of France. After a long series of battles the English were finally forced to withdraw almost completely from France after the Battle of Castillion in 1453.

Almost immediately the country embarked on the Wars of the Roses (1455-87), this was a long-drawn out civil war for possession of the crown of England. The battles were fought between the House of Lancaster and the House of York. At the Battle of Bosworth in 1485 King Richard III lost his kingdom and his life to the victorious Henry Tudor, who was crowned Henry VII.

During the age of the Tudors England assumed a previously unmatched importance in Europe in political, cultural, and artistic terms. One of the greatest palaces, Hampton Court Palace was built and developed by the Tudor monarchs. Under King Henry VIII the religious complexion of the country was changed when he renounced the Roman Catholic church in favour of Protestantism. During this period all the abbeys and monasteries were dissolved and many of the buildings destroyed. However, many romantic ruins still remain around the country, such as Glastonbury, Fountains, and

Rievaux abbies. Years of brutal religious suppression followed until Queen Elizabeth I unified the country.

Another significant advance was the exploration across the Atlantic to the New World of the Americas. The first colonies failed, but slowly and surely settlements succeeded and a whole new world began. Crisis loomed as Elizabeth aged because, due to her political manoeuvring, she had not married, so she had no direct issue to pass on the throne. Instead she left it to a distant Stuart cousin, King James VI, who unified the throne by also becoming King James I of England. This united England and Scotland for the first time in history though the official Act of Parliament (the Act of Union) was not passed until 1707, another hundred years when the permanent union made the country into Great Britain.

Religion was still a contentious issue in Britain, as it was across Europe, and religious persecution was prevalent. In August 1620 some religious dissenters left Southampton dock on the Mayflower, intent on finding a new life free from the established church. They had to put in for repairs at Plymouth before embarking on the long Atlantic crossing, to land at Plymouth Rock, in the territory that would later become known as Massachusetts. They were not the first settlers in the New World, but they are the most famous.

Like their ancestors before them, the Stuart monarchs believed in the Divine Right of Kings, which in simplified form meant that nobody could challenge the king's will on any matter whatsoever. In an increasingly egalitarian world the Stuarts found their divine right to rule

increasingly resented and challenged by Parliament and the people. The struggle for supremacy between Parliament and the king as to who really ruled the country led to bitter civil war between the Cavaliers (Royalists) and Roundheads (Parliamentarians) of the New Model Army in 1641. The king, Charles I, was eventually defeated, captured, tried, and publicly beheaded in Whitehall in 1649.

For the first time Britain had an elected leader in the shape of the Puritan Oliver Cromwell who led the country through the auspices of Parliament. As Lord Protector (a title granted him in 1653) Cromwell ruled autocratically with supreme legislative and executive power. He wielded a fist of iron and all public as well as private frivolity was banned on pain of death. When he died in 1658 he was succeeded by his son, who was so unpopular that within the year Parliament, sick of years of punitive restrictions and financial chaos, invited

the son of Charles I to come back and take the throne.

So Britain resumed its monarchy under Charles II in 1660. This period, known as the Restoration, brought back music and entertainment to the land; however the monarch was increasingly beholden to Parliament to grant his desires and by the time William of Orange (William III) became king, parliamentary rule was properly established. The basis of the modern political parties emerged with the Whigs and Tories. A succession of dull German kings ensued and their unpopularity in the New World lost them the American colonies after the War of Independence in 1775-83. In 1801 the legislative union of Great Britain and Ireland was implemented and the country became the United Kingdom of Great Britain and Ireland. Not long after, in 1837 a young girl of eighteen, named Victoria, succeeded to the throne after her father and then uncle (William IV) died. Under her the impetus of the Industrial Revolution took Britain to the forefront of world supremacy. The British Empire was established and British Empire-builders left their homelands to explore and subjugate foreign lands. In the 1890s one person in every four on earth was a subject of Queen Victoria. British society as a whole became more urban as people left the land to work in the growing cities. By the time Victoria died in 1901 Great Britain was the most powerful country in the world with an economy to match. Many British cities had their biggest growth period under her rule and much of the housing and public buildings across the land date from her era.

The global pre-eminence of the British Empire lasted until the devastating human and economic destruction of World Wars I and II decimated the country's economy and labour base. In 1921 after World War I, Ireland was partitioned into the Republic and the six northern Irish counties, and the kingdom was renamed accordingly as the United Kingdom of Great Britain and Northern Ireland in 1927. In they years following, the once mighty British Empire has been largely peacefully dismantled, with countries being given back their own destinies to decide. Many of them chose to remain loosely affiliated through the institution of the Commonwealth. In 1999 Scotland and Wales were both granted their own independent legislative bodies.

In 1953 a new Elizabethan age started with Queen Elizabeth II; the nation took new heart and slowly started to rebuild. In the last decades of the millennium the economy has slowly rebuilt and new projects and ideas are revolutionising the country. It may not be as powerful as it was a century ago but it is still a green and pleasant land.

WEST COUNTRY

Cornwall Coast ▼

The beautiful south Cornwall coast cannot fail to inspire. All along the Fowey, Fal, and Helford estuaries you can walk in the footsteps of great novelists such as Daphne du Maurier and dynamic world leaders like General Eisenhower. Discover the history, industrial archaeology, shipwrecks, and legends of these hidden places.

ENGLAND

WEST COUNTRY

The scenic beauty of the West Country knows no equal. In the far south-west lies Cornwall with its subtropical gardens and fantastic coastline, and Devon, the epitome of rural England, with thatched villages and patchwork fields. Further east lies the rural county of Dorset with its wonderful pebble and sand beaches, pretty cob-walled houses, quiet lanes and tranquillity. North lie the hills and Levels of Somerset with lush orchards and rolling hills, while to the east are the chalk hills of Wiltshire with numerous prehistoric sites and vast expanses of skyline.

Wiltshire contains the World Heritage Site of Stonehenge and the national Ridgeway. Said to be Europe's oldest road, it cuts through the county and passes another World Heritage Site at Avebury where the stone circle is one of the world's most important monuments. Wiltshire has the highest concentration of prehistoric sites in Europe. It also has many chalk figures cut into the hillsides. Legend has it that the oldest, the Westbury White Horse, was cut as a memorial to one of King Arthur's victories over the Danes. Much of the county is designated as Areas of Outstanding Natural Beauty.

Dorset has a rich and varied scenery. In the east, most of the land is low lying with extensive heathlands; in the centre expanses of chalk downland as far as the eye can see lead to the west, which is more hilly with a rich landscape of woodland and small fields. The north of Dorset is dominated by a plain, known as the Blackmore Vale. Dorset has some of the prettiest villages in England—as well as the longest, Piddletrenthide that stretches for some three miles along the River Piddle. The county also includes the newest "village" in England—at Poundbury where the Prince of Wales is creating a "model" community on the edge of the lovely old county town of Dorchester. Nearby, visit Thomas Hardy's cottage and some ten miles away at Cloud's Hill, Bovington, Lawrence of Arabia's even smaller cottage.

The Dorset and East Devon coast has just been designated a World Heritage Site for its amazing prehistoric rocks. Nicknamed the Jurassic Coast, a walk along the route will take the visitor through millennia of geological rocks. At Lyme Regis and Charmouth fossils lie scattered on the beaches and at other points along the walk huge fossils lie embedded into the rocks, including remnants of a fossilised forest.

Devon is a very rural county with most local business still revolving around agriculture and the sea. One of the glories of Devon is Dartmoor National Park, which provides some of the most stunning landscapes in Britain, the open wild spaces contrasting with the picture postcard scenery of small, thatched villages set in wooded valleys and open countryside. On top of the moors sit imposing towering rocks called "Tors" which are the stumps of ancient volcanoes.

Nearby the county town of Exeter is located around a beautiful Norman cathedral surrounded by a quiet cathedral close. The city also contains a university which attracts students from around the world. In south Devon, on the border with Cornwall, lies the old port of Plymouth from which the Pilgrim Fathers sailed on their journey to the New World and Sir Francis Drake set out to attack the Spanish Armada.

The Somerset countryside captures the essence of rural England. It is still a very agricultural county of rolling hills, peaceful wooded river valleys, and scenic villages. The five sets of hills—the Blackdowns, Mendips, Quantocks, Poldens, and the Brendons—all have their own special character. The flat Somerset Levels are probably the most important wetland area in England. The meadows and flower-filled fields are home to an enormous variety of wading birds, wildfowl, and butterflies, and are now designated as an environmentally sensitive area.

Of all the western counties Cornwall is the wildest and most unforgiving. Craggy rocks and bent trees are proof to the searing winter winds which scream in from across the Atlantic. Cornwall truly feels ancient: wayside crosses and holy wells greet travellers on their journey through the county. The Cornish are proud Celts and their heritage is still obvious.

Around the coast especially, but inland as well, stand the tall chimneys of old tin mines signalling a once important mining industry. Other remainders of old Cornish industry are the spent hills of china clay spoil around Camborne and Redruth—silent testament to the toil that went into extracting a living from Cornwall's rocks. One such old open cast mine has been turned into the amazing Eden Project, a series of huge geodesic domes that contain plants from around the world, providing different climates and ecosystems.

ENGLAND

CORNISH COAST ▲

The long-distance South-West Coastal Path starts in Dorset and—as its name suggests—winds its way around the coastline of Dorset, Devon, Cornwall, and Somerset from Poole to Minehead. It passes through wonderful places: Lulworth Cove and Durdle Door; the latest British World Heritage Site, the fossil-rich environs of Lyme Regis; the sunken river valleys of south Devon—the Exe, Teign, Dart, and Kingsbridge Estuary; the beautiful craggy coast of Cornwall including the southernmost tip of England, Lizard Point and the cliffs of Land's End; Merlin's Cave at Tintagel, where King Arthur was born; the surfing beaches of the north coast, such as Widemouth Bay and Woolacombe; and then the edges of Exmoor.

ST IVES ◀

A popular tourist destination, St Ives incorporates a traditional fishing harbor and a popular holiday centre. The magnificent resort is famed for its safe beaches, the azure blue sea of the bay, its tiny cobbled streets, and hidden corners waiting to be explored.

St Ives ▲

Cornish buildings are traditionally built of local granite and slate-roofed. They need to be solidly built to withstand the extremes of Atlantic weather that regularly lash this spectacular far-western peninsula.

Hayle Bay ▶

Polzeath can be found in the Camel Estuary in Hayle Bay. The long flat beach is very popular with surfers and bathers alike.

ENGLAND

PENDENNIS CASTLE ◀

Pendennis Castle is part of the coastal defences built by King Henry VIII when England was under threat of invasion from the Continent. It sits guarding Falmouth Bay opposite its twin castle, St Mawes on the other shore. Pendennis Castle has defended the anchorage of the Carrick Roads for over 450 years. Today you revisit the castle's history from Tudor times to the refortification work in both world wars when it was used as a barracks and part of the western coastal defences against invasion.

ST MAWES CASTLE ▶

On one side of the River Fal guarding Falmouth Bay sits St Mawes Castle, built by Henry VIII as a small artillery fort at the same time as Pendennis Castle on the opposite shore. St Mawes is shaped like a clover leaf with three massive circular lobes. On the outer wall of the keep are coats of arms and ornamental inscriptions. St Mawes has been used as a barracks and was part of the coastal defence system during the 20th century wars when England was threatened with invasion from the Continent.

ST MICHAEL'S MOUNT ◀

The jewel in Cornwall's crown, St Michael's Mount has been the home of the St Aubyn family for 300 years since the Civil War. The Mount sits well into Mount's Bay and is separated from the mainland and the small town of Marazion by a 500-yard long natural granite causeway, only reachable by boat when the tide is in. At the centre of the building is a medieval church that has long been a place of pilgrimage. It is a popular tourist destination as it captures all the magic of Cornwall.

BERRY HEAD ▶

Twelve guns were put here during the American War of Independence, but were removed when peace came in 1783. Just ten years later, when England was yet again at war with France, guns were redeployed around the town.

BRIXHAM HARBOUR ▼

A replica of the *Golden Hind*, flagship of Sir. Francis Drake, is a living museum in Brixham harbour in south Devon. This small fishing town still depends on the sea for its livelihood.

BROWNSEA ISLAND ▲

Brownsea Island is the largest island in Poole harbour and is owned by the National Trust. It contains a 200-acre nature reserve on the north side used by a wide range of coastal wading birds.

PAIGNTON SEAFRONT ◄

Paignton pier stretches out into Lyme Bay and was originally built by the Victorians for the many visitors to this popular seaside town. The mansion in the heart of Paignton has 15 acres of ornamental gardens laid out in the early 1900s devised by the French garden designer Achille Duchene.

TORRE ABBEY ▶

Torre Abbey was built in 1196 near the sea front at Torquay as a monastery. After Henry VIII's Dissolution of the Monasteries it became a private house and was extensively rebuilt in the 18th century. In the grounds are medieval ruins, a tithe barn, and the famous Torre Abbey meadows. The abbey is now a museum featuring a fine art display. Nearby Torre Abbey sands is a large and popular beach, with a windsurfing school and plenty of nearby cafes.

TORQUAY ◀

Torquay is Devon's most popular tourist resort. There is a large marina and harbour at its centre with facilities for watersports such as sailing, jet-skiing, and windsurfing. Thatcher's Rock, off the coast at Torquay serves as home for a colony of seabirds and can be viewed from the shore or by means of a boat trip from the harbour. Torquay is renowned for its picturesque walks, many with breath-taking views over the ocean. Nearby beaches include Ansteys Cove, Watcombe, Babbacombe, and Oddicombe with its cliff railway.

COCKINGTON ▶

Cockington is named after the de Cockington family who owned the manor from 1130 until 1350. Cockington is in Domesday Book a traditional country estate, complete with manor house, beautiful church which was restored in 1882, formal gardens, pretty thatched village houses, water-wheel, woodlands, meadows, and pasture. Cricket is played in front of the manor house on Sundays and is a venue for various concerts and entertaining events at other times.

ENGLAND

AMERICAN MUSEUM
CLAVERTON MANOR ▲

Not far from the city of Bath is the American Museum in Britain. Inside is chronicled everything about early American lifestyle, artifacts, and culture, dating from the New England colonists right through to the Civil War period. One of the main features is a replica of George Washington's garden at Mount Vernon, as well an American arboretum. The museum has a substantial collection of fine American hand-made quilts.

ROMAN BATHS AND BATH ABBEY
◀

The Romans called Bath "Aquae Sulis" in honour of the spa waters found there. In the centre of the city lie the Roman Baths—among the best preserved Roman remains anywhere in England. The main pool is open to the sky and is below the modern street level. The Baths were "lost" for centuries until rediscovered in 1879. The Baths adjoin the 18th century Pump Rooms and Bath Abbey nearby. A monastery was founded on the site of the Abbey c.800, however the present building was started in 1499 and, after damage during the Dissolution, extensively restored in the early 1600s and again between 1860 and 1883.

ROYAL CRESCENT AND THE CIRCUS ▶

The World Heritage city of Bath is the most complete and best preserved Georgian city in Britain. It became highly fashionable to take the waters here in the 18th century when fashionable society flocked to the city. John Wood the Elder designed the Circus which was begun in 1754. In turn his son, John Wood the Younger, designed the Royal Crescent. This is a sweeping semi-elipse of 30 houses facing a large sloping lawn and is one of the great architectural features of this city full of spectacular buildings.

PULTENEY BRIDGE ▶

English Palladian architecture at its best, Pulteney Bridge provides the perfect link between two halves of a Palladian city. The bridge was commissioned by William Johnston Pulteney and designed by Robert Adam. It was completed in 1773 with 11 small shops along either side and was designed to take passengers over the River Avon to a planned new Palladian development of an area of meadows which would be called Bathwick. However, the American War of Independance frightened investors and Adam's original classical plans were subsequently much changed.

ENGLAND

IFORD MANOR BRADFORD-ON-AVON ◀
Set in a lovely small town full of beautiful buildings, Iford Manor is a Tudor house with a classical facade.

FIVE-ARCHED RAILWAY BRIDGE ▲
The bridge at Creech St Michael in Somerset carried the Bristol and Exeter Railway to Chard over the River Tone. It was built in 1863 at the height of railway expansion. The line closed in 1962 and the bridge is no longer in use.

SS GREAT BRITAIN ▲ ▲
Designed by Isambard Kingdom Brunel, it was built in Bristol 1843.

ROMAN MOSAIC ◀
Part of a Roman mosaic pavement (dating from c. 360AD) found in a newly discovered villa at Lopen, near Ilminster, Somerset. English Heritage is surveying and recording the site. It measures almost 33ft by 20ft.

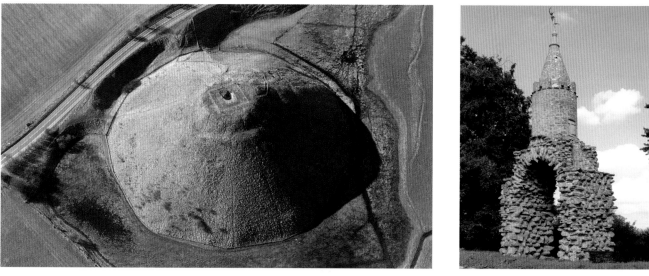

SILBURY HILL ▲

Silbury Hill is the largest artificial prehistoric mound in Western Europe, one of a very rare class of monuments called "Monumental Mounds."

JACK THE TREACLE EATER
BARWICK PARK ▼

A Grade II listed folly dating from around 1775. The coarse rubble arch is topped with a round tower which in turn is crowned with a winged Mercury. The tower appears to have a door, which has been blocked up. According to local legend Jack was a local runner who carried family messages to London.

STONEHENGE ▲

Stonehenge is Britain's greatest prehistoric monument and a World Heritage Site. Built in three phases between 3050BC and 1600BC, it stands at the centre of a ceremonial landscape containing 450 scheduled ancient monuments of national importance.

LONGLEAT ▶

Longleat in Wiltshire is regarded as the finest example of high Elizabethan architecture in Britain, and is one of the most beautiful stately homes open to the public. Longleat was built for Sir John Thynne and he entertained Queen Elizabeth I there in 1575. The building has been extended and remodelled over the centuries. In the late 18th century "Capability" Brown landscaped the park by removing the previous formal gardens.

SOUTH OF ENGLAND

WINDSOR CASTLE

Started by William the Conqueror in about 1078 to guard the approaches to London, Windsor Castle has been considerably added to over the centuries. Most of the present fabric, however, dates from the 19th century. It is the largest castle in England, enclosing nearly 13 acres. Windsor Castle was a favorite residence of Queen Victoria and is still used regularly by the royal family.

SOUTH OF ENGLAND

OXFORD UNIVERSITY ◀

Oxford is a unique and historic teaching institution. As the oldest English-speaking university in the world, it lays claim to eight centuries of continuous existence. There is no clear date of foundation, but teaching existed at Oxford in some form in 1096 and developed rapidly from 1167, when Henry II banned English students from attending the University of Paris.

OSBORNE HOUSE ▶

Built by Queen Victoria between 1845 and 1851 as a country retreat where she and her family could be free from state ceremonial. Today, the drawing, dining, and billiard rooms and the private apartments are laid out almost exactly as they were in her day. To mark the centenary of Victoria's death, English Heritage has restored two of Osborne House's most important rooms—the dining room and the banqueting hall.

The south of England is a mix of three contrasting regions: the Thames and Chilterns country through which the great River Thames flows, the coast, and the Downs. The Thames winds its way through pretty towns and villages as well as through the royal town of Windsor with its imposing castle. Further north lies the ancient university town of Oxford and some of the most famous stately homes in Britain.

The Thames Path and the Ridgeway National Trails are ideal for walking, and cycling, with plenty of canalside and towpath routes. Always popular in summer, the Thames throngs with activity and there are plenty of riverside restaurants, pubs, and cafes for that welcome sit down and rest.

Just south of London lie the North Downs and towards the coast, the South Downs. These beautiful green rolling hills and picturesque woodlands, with friendly historic market towns. The entire area is renowned for its heritage , from the medieval city of Winchester with its famous cathedral to stately homes and houses, like Highclere Castle, near Newbury, or smaller properties with literary connections such as Jane Austen's House, in Chawton near Alton in Hampshire.

The region is particularly known for its fishing rivers, especially the Itchen and Test, attracting enthusiasts from around the world.

The south coast has a reputation for its safe, sand or pebble beaches and sunshine. The coast is also home to major maritime attractions such as the *Mary Rose* and HMS *Victory*, Admiral Nelson's flagship. Ancient forts and castles line the coastline, see Roman Portchester near Portsmouth or Carisbrooke on the Isle of Wight. Take a short ferry ride and discover the island's timeless delights, and be sure to visit Queen Victoria's holiday home, Osborne House.

THE NEEDLES ▶

A series of rock formations off the western point of the Isle of Wight, the Needles Lighthouse was manned until 1997.

HARTING DOWN ▼

211 hectares of woodland and chalk downland owned by the National Trust. The site is grazed using traditional techniques to encourage the regrowth of downland species.

HINTON AMPNER GARDEN ▲

One of the great gardens of the 20th century, this masterpiece of design is by Ralph Dutton, eighth and last Lord Sherborne.

J.F. KENNEDY AND U.S. AIR FORCES MEMORIALS ▼

These memorials are set in an acre of England near the River Thames at Runnymede, Middlesex, given to the American people by the people of England.

MOTTISFONT ABBEY GARDEN ▲

Set in glorious countryside along the River Test, this 12th century Augustinian priory was converted into a private house after the Dissolution of the Monasteries.

RUNNYMEDE ▼

This attractive area of riverside meadows, grassland, and broadleaved woodland, is rich in diverse flora and fauna, and part-designated a Site of Special Scientific Interest.

THE VYNE ▲

Built in the early 16th century for Lord Sandys, Henry VIII's Lord Chamberlain, the house acquired a classical portico in the mid-17th century (the first of its kind in England) and contains a fascinating Tudor chapel with Renaissance glass, a Palladian staircase, a wealth of old panelling and fine furniture.

UPPARK ▲

A fine late 17th-century house set high on the South Downs with magnificent sweeping views to the sea. The complete servants' quarters in the basement are shown as they were in Victorian days when H.G. Wells' mother was housekeeper.

BLENHEIM PALACE AND GARDENS ▼

The birthplace of Sir Winston Churchill, Blenheim Palace was designed by John Vanbrugh. John Churchill was the first Duke of Marlborough in 1702. He was a military genius and won many battles, one being near the small town of Blenheim in 1704. For this famous victory Queen Anne gave him Marlborough and the Royal Manor of Woodstock.

SOUTH-EAST ENGLAND

HAMPTON COURT ▼

A riot of colour, the gardens of Hampton Court are always worth visiting but especially when the annual flower show takes place. Originally sponsored by Network Southeast the show was bought by the Royal Horticultural Society and has become one of the major events of the horticultural year attracting thousands of eager gardeners and would-be gardeners.

SOUTH-EAST ENGLAND

The south-east of England covers the four counties of Kent, Surrey, and East and West Sussex. The region contains over 500 miles of long-distance footpaths and cycle routes over some of the best landscapes in England, through chalk downland, wooded valleys, and dramatic cliff tops,. Over 250 miles of coastline offers everything from traditional bucket-and-spade family seaside holidays to romantic breaks.

Nicknamed "London by the Sea", Brighton is the most cosmopolitan city in the south of England. Along its seafront stand magnificent Regency buildings and two great piers that jut out into the English Channel. Behind the main esplanade lies one of the most exotic buildings in the country—the Brighton Pavilion, built by the Prince Regent in elaborate Chinese style with absolutely no expense spared.

Kent is an enchanting county full of beautiful gardens, a wonderful coastline, quaint villages, and bustling towns, all set in delightful countryside. There are many magnificent stately homes and castles to enjoy—none more romantic than lovely Leeds Castle, considered by many to be the loveliest castle in the world. Scotney Castle is another beautiful old building, surrounded by the most romantic garden in England.

Kent is distinguished by its many oast houses, the traditional buildings in which hops for beer making were dried. Travel through the countryside and you'll see delightful orchards and hop gardens—full of white and pink blossom in the spring and then laden with fruit later in the summer.

With its proximity to London the county of Surrey is full of historic interest. The magnificent River Thames flows through on its way to London and riverside walks are one of the highlights of the county. The Magna Carta was signed at Runnymede on the Thames in 1215 between King John and the Barons of England and is lauded as the birthplace of British democracy. Despite this Surrey has some of the finest royal residences anywhere—none bigger or better than Hampton Court Palace, famously the home of King Henry VIII and his six wives.

Over one third of Surrey has been designated an Area of .Outstanding Natural Beauty. The county is full of rolling hills and

DOVER CASTLE ▲
Sited strategically above the town, much of the castle was built by King Henry II.

LEEDS CASTLE ▶
Listed in the Domesday Book, this castle has been a Norman stronghold, a residence for six of England's medieval queens, and a rural retreat for the powerful and influential.

breathtaking views, in addition there are many fantastic gardens such as the Royal Horticultural Society's gardens at Wisley and the world-renowned Botanical Gardens at Kew. Surrey also has great horse racing at Kempton Park, Epsom Downs, and Sandown Racecourse.

Sussex has 90 miles of coastline along the English Channel and much of the county is protected as an Area of Outstanding Natural Beauty. The ancient chalk South Downs are famous for walking, wildlife, and the Seven Sisters cliffs. Sussex also has more than it share of buildings of special historic interest, places such Arundel, Bodiam, Herstmonceux, and Pevensey castles, and Battle Abbey to name but a few.

ENGLAND

HEVER CASTLE ◀

Hever Castle dates back to the 13th century and is best known as the childhood home of Henry VIII's second wife, Anne Boleyn. The family's fortunes declined after her execution and the Crown appropriated the castle. It survived more or less intact as a working farmhouse until 1903 when it was bought by William Waldorf Astor. He spared no expense to refurbish the castle and transform its gardens into a Mediterranean style extravaganza.

BODIAM CASTLE ◀

Built in 1385 by Sir Edward Dalyngrygge, Bodiam Castle is square and surrounded by a broad moat. The castle was attacked in 1484, and again in the Civil War, when it fell to Parliamentary forces. They were ordered to dismantle it and the castle was left as a ruin for centuries. Lord Curzon bought it in 1917, and spent a fortune on restoring it to a beautiful ruin of the quintessential romantic castle.

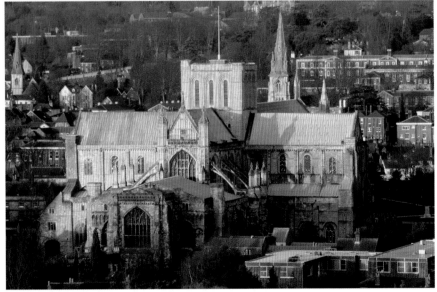

CANTERBURY CATHEDRAL ◀

For at least 1,400 years the worship of God has been offered on the site of this cathedral. It was the first Gothic cathedral to be built in Britain and during medieval times in particular, was a major centre for pilgrims, especially to pay homage at the shrine of Sir Thomas à Becket.

WINCHESTER CATHEDRAL ▶

A Norman cathedral largely redesigned in the 14th century, Winchester cathedral was built as a show of Norman power as well as spirituality to reinforce the new rule on the population of England.

ENGLAND

ALFRISTON CLERGY HOUSE ◀

The Old Clergy House dates from about 1350. In 1896 it became the first building to be purchased by the National Trust—at a cost of £10. The substantial church dates back to the 14th century and is often called the "Cathedral of the Downs". The mound on which it stands is thought to have been a pagan burial-place. The green in front of the church is known as the Tye. There has been a settlement at Alfriston for centuries, and the village boasts many fine 15th century buildings. It was once notorious as a centre for smugglers.

STANDEN HOUSE ◀

A family house built in the 1890s, Standen was designed by Philip Webb, a friend of William Morris. A showpiece of the Arts & Crafts Movement, it is decorated throughout with Morris carpets, fabrics, and wallpapers, and contemporary paintings, tapestries, and furniture.

CLAREMONT GARDENS ◀

Begun in 1715 the creation and development of these gardens involved some of the greatest names in garden history, including Sir John Vanbrugh, Charles Bridgeman, William Kent, and "Capability" Brown. The first gardens were begun in about 1715 and in the 19th century the delights of Claremont were famed throughout Europe. Since 1975 the National Trust has been restoring this earlier scheme following years of sad neglect.

WISLEY GARDENS ▶

A very beautiful garden with romantic half-timbered Tudor-style buildings, Wisley is now run by the Royal Horticultural Society. There is a canal designed by Sir Geoffrey Jellicoe, a rock garden, formal and walled gardens by Lanning Roper, herbaceous borders, rose garden, summer garden, winter garden, and woodland garden, a fruit field, glasshouses, and an arboretum. Then there are the alpine gardens, the model vegetable gardens, and a new country garden by Penelope Hobhouse.

HAMPTON COURT ◀

For almost 200 years, Hampton Court Palace was at the centre of court life, politics, and national history. Although often identified with Henry VIII, its history was influenced just as much by William III and Queen Mary II in the late 17th century. (See also page 30-31).

RIVER WEY ▶

Narrow-boat holidays are generally quiet and reflective—particularly if you live in the bustling Home Counties. Surrey is better known for its intensive commuter-belt road and rail system, but the Wey Navigation which stretches over 20 miles through the heart of the county. This inland waterway, uniquely, is owned by the National Trust thus ensuring it against unsympathetic development and preserving its historic locks and keepers' cottages.

ENGLAND

POLESDEN LACEY ◄

Begun in 1824 to designs by Thomas Cubitt, the house has been greatly enlarged over the years and the opulent rooms contain many treasures.

NYMANS GARDENS ►

One of the great gardens of the Sussex Weald, Nymans still retains much of its distinctive family style in the historic collection of plants, shrubs, and trees. This is reflected in the surrounding estate, with its woodland walks and wild garden, and in the many rare and exotic species collected from overseas.

HAM HOUSE ► ▲

An outstanding Stuart house, built in 1610 and then enlarged in the 1670s when it was at the heart of Restoration court life and intrigue.

CISSBURY RING ◄

This great prehistoric hill fort built by Iron Age people sits high up on the Sussex Downs and still has the remains of a vast defensive wall enclosing an area of 65 acres. The inner band is over a mile round and protected what was probably a tribal capital.

HATCHLANDS, EAST CLANDON ◄

The house was built in the 1750s for Admiral Boscawen, hero of the Battle of Louisburg, and set in a beautiful Repton Park offering a variety of park and woodland walks.

PENSHURST PLACE ►

The garden of Penshurst Place is the oldest in private ownership, with records dating back to the 14th century. It was a favourite spot of royalty—in the form of —Henry VIII in the 16th century. The house, however, was built by a wealthy retired merchant from London who wanted to be the lord of the manor.

LONDON

NIGHT VIEW OF THE CITY OF LONDON ▼

The River Thames is one of the great glories of London, enjoyed by Londoners and visitors alike. There is a riverside path almost all the way from the Thames Barrier to Windsor and every section has something of interest. One particularly glorious stretch—the Millennium Mile—runs on the opposite bank to the City of London from the London Eye, past St Paul's Cathedral, the Globe Theatre, the new Millennium Bridge, and on to the Tower of London and Tower Bridge.

ENGLAND

LONDON

The saying goes that "he who is tired of London is tired of life" and it is hard to disagree when the seemingly inexhaustible attractions of the capital city are examined—the great buildings, the parks, the shopping, the museums, the Thames: all are well worth exploring.

London was founded by the Romans around AD43 at the furthest point up the Thames that their ships could easily reach on the tide. The Roman town occupied very much the same area as the square mile of the City today. When William the Conqueror arrived in 1066 the City of London was still contained within the Roman walls and was by then the most important settlement in England. King Edward the Confessor had built his palace and a great abbey at Westminster. The Normans changed the look of London forever by centring their capital on the imposing Tower of London.

As London grew in importance so the wooden buildings and tight, narrow streets grew more numerous. This led to disaster in September 1666 when an oven caught fire in Pudding Lane (a site marked today by the Monument). The fire spread rapidly through the wooden buildings until a total of 13,000 houses had been destroyed. Amazingly, only four people were killed in what became known as the Great Fire of London. A law was passed that all new buildings had to be built from stone or brick. Plans were immediately drawn up to rebuild the city with Sir Christopher Wren's designs

▶ **BUCKINGHAM PALACE**
The official London residence of Britain's sovereigns since 1837, the palace evolved from a town house that was owned from the beginning of the 18th century by the Dukes of Buckingham.

primarily chosen. He designed the new St Paul's on the site of the destroyed 7th century building, and collaborated on building more churches around the city.

The next main change to the face of London was the arrival of the railways that created a huge wave of development in the late 1800s. But the biggest changes to London would start when it was pounded by the Luftwaffe in World War II. The vast docklands area, was badly hit, ending London's role as a great port. Rebuilding the city took place rapidly after the war but it took until the 1980s before the revival started in Docklands and old docks were removed or converted into housing and retail areas. During the late 1990s the entire City of London has undergone a vast rebuilding. Londoners at last are able to fully enjoy their magnificent river as walkways and other amenities have been developed along the riverside.

One of the most successful attractions is the British Airways London Eye, opposite the Houses of Parliament. The wheel almost imperceptibly revolves to show the visitor stunning views over London to the distant hills beyond. Its most startling revelation perhaps is to show just how green a city London actually is, filled with tree-lined roads, garden squares, and lots of parks.

ENGLAND

London contains the oldest museum in the world, the British Museum. Across London, South Kensington is home to the Natural History Museum, the Science Museum, and the Victoria & Albert Museum. Furthermore London is home to one of the largest contemporary art galleries in the world: Tate Modern. The National Gallery and neighbouring National Portrait Gallery are a must for any art-lover.

London contains three World Heritage Sites: Westminster Palace, Abbey, and Saint Margaret's Church; the Tower of London; and the area designated Maritime Greenwich, where the National Observatory was located and the world meridian timeline starts.

HOUSES OF PARLIAMENT ▶
The site of the Houses of Parliament is the Palace of Westminster, one a royal palace and former residence of kings. The layout of today's building is intricate, with nearly 1,200 rooms, 100 staircases and well over two miles of passages.

ROYAL ALBERT HALL ▶
Following the success of the Great Exhibition of 1851 (the world's first international "Expo"), the Hall was conceived by Albert, the Prince Consort, as the centerpiece of the proposed development of a range of national institutions—cultural, scientific, and academic—that for the first time would be located on a single site.

GREAT CLOCK OF WESTMINSTER ◀
At 9ft diameter, 7½ft high, and weighing 13 tons 10 cwt 3 qtr 15lb (13,760kg), the hour bell of the Great Clock of Westminster—known worldwide as "Big Ben"—is the most famous bell ever cast at Whitechapel.

ENGLAND

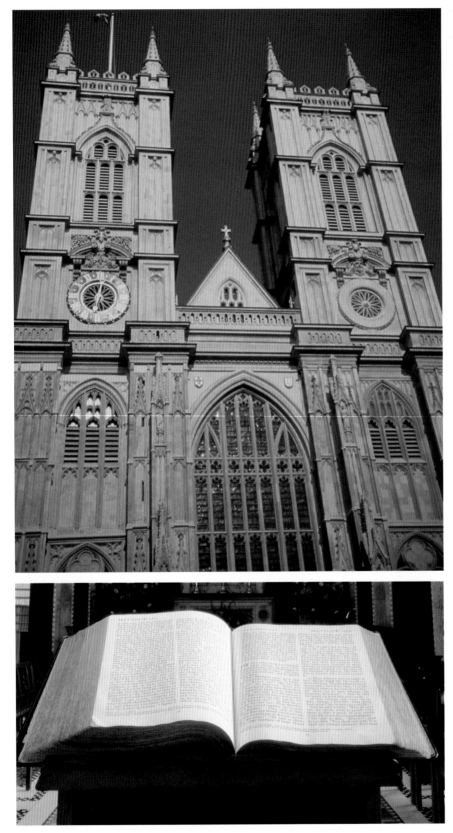

WESTMINSTER ABBEY ◄
A site of holy buildings since the 7th century, King William the Conqueror was crowned here on 28 December 1065 and it has been the setting for every coronation since and for numerous other royal occasions. Inside lies Edward the Confessor's Shrine, plus the tombs of kings and queens, and countless memorials to the famous. Geoffrey Chaucer is buried here—so are Ben Jonson, John Dryden, Alfred, Lord Tennyson, Sir Isaac Newton, Robert Stephenson, and Thomas Telford.

ST PAUL'S CATHEDRAL ►
In 604, the original St Paul's Cathedral was just a small wooden church. By 1220, St Paul's Cathedral had burnt down three times, each time being rebuilt. During the Great Fire, St Paul's Cathedral was completely destroyed. The rebuilding of St Paul's was finished in 1708 by Sir Christopher Wren and is regarded as his masterpiece.

TOWER OF LONDON ►
Her Majesty's Tower of London is situated in East London on the boundaries of the borough of Stepney and the City of London. This, the most perfect medieval fortress in Britain, was begun by William the Conqueror and added to by successive monarchs. It has been a palace, a prison, a zoo, a mint, and a place of execution. The Crown Jewels are still closely guarded inside its walls.

THE HOLY BIBLE ◄
ST. PAUL'S CATHEDRAL

TOWER BRIDGE ◀ ▶

Built in the Gothic style, Tower Bridge
is one of the great icons of London. It
was designed by the architect Sir
Horace Jones and the engineer John
Wolfe-Barry. Unfortunately the former
died a year into the project and it was
not completed to his original specifica-
tion. Work was started in 1881 and
finally finished 13 years later. It was
opened in 1894 with great ceremony
by the Prince of Wales. It is the most
famous example of a bascule bridge in
the world and crosses the River Thames
in the heart of London. The towers
have a steel framework clad in stone in
order to support the great weight of
the bascules. Hidden inside are also lifts
to take pedestrians to the high-level
footbridge.

WINSTON CHURCHILL ▶

Ivor Roberts-Jones sculpted this bronze
study of Sir Winston Churchill in 1973.
It stands 12 feet high in Parliament
Square and faces the Houses of
Parliament where Churchill gave many
of his most inspiring speeches. It shows
him striding out in typically aggressive
pose.

COUNTY HALL ▲

Building work on County Hall began in 1912 to provide a home for the offices of the London County Council. More recently the L.C.C. became the G.L.C. (Greater London Council), an elected body whose job it was to run London. It has since been converted into luxury appartments and Hotels.

MARBLE ARCH AT NIGHT ◀

John Nash designed the Marble Arch, like much else of elegance in London. It was built in 1828 as the chief entrance to Buckingham Palace, but when the Palace was extended in 1851, the Arch was moved to its current site as an entrance to Hyde Park. By tradition, only senior members of the royal family, the King's Troop and the Royal Horse Artillery are allowed to ride or drive through the Arch.

QUEEN ELIZABETH GATE ▶

Commonly known as Queen Mother's Gate. Built in 1993, this elaborate gate was sculpted for the Queen Mother who was a sprightly 93 years old at the time.

EAST OF ENGLAND

The East of England is based around the ancient kingdom of East Anglia, originally made up of the North Folk (Norfolk) and the South Folk (Suffolk). Today Cambridgeshire, Bedfordshire, Essex and Hertfordshire join these counties as belonging to the East of England. The area is epitomised by gentle landscapes straight from an 18th century oil painting, with villages of pretty half-timbered cottages, cities brimming with history and culture, magnificent stately homes and huge cathedrals. Along the coast lie traditional seaside resorts. Up by the fens the land is very flat giving magnificent views of huge open skies reflected in the numerous lazy rivers and

lakes. This is a delightful unspoilt unassuming area, ideal for boating and fishing and really enjoying the outdoor life.

Queen Elizabeth II has a large country estate at Sandringham where she spends as much time as possible. Nearby lies England's only working lavender farm, while in South Holland the fields are alive with seasonal flowers, fruit orchards, and wayside stalls of fresh vegetables. The town of Spalding is famous for its horticultural products, in particular its spectacular bulb fields.

Royalty has strong connections with the area. At Buckden Towers Katherine of Aragon, the first wife of Henry VIII, was kept before finally being imprisoned

at Kimbolton Castle in 1533. After her death, she was buried at Peterborough Cathedral as was Mary, Queen of Scots, before being moved to Westminster Abbey. In Castle Rising, Queen Isabella, the "she-wolf of France' was banished by Edward III for her part in the murder of her husband Edward II. Newmarket was "discovered" by James I as a horse racing center —and established by Charles II as the horse racing capital of England. Castle Hedingham is a Norman castle where the massive keep was home of the Earls of Oxford for more than 400 years and was visited by kings Henry VII, VIII, and Queen Elizabeth I, as well as being besieged by King John.

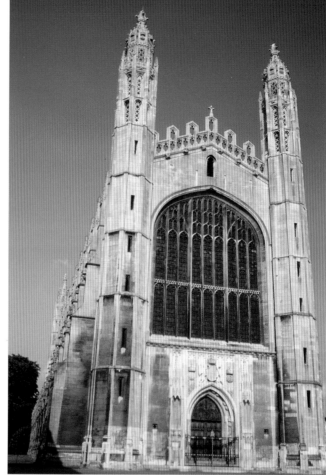

CAMBRIDGE ◀ AND ▲

Cambridge manages to combine its role as an historic city with an ancient university and, in recent years, an internationally acknowledged center of excellence for technology and science.

KINGS COLLEGE CHAPEL ◥

Henry VI was only 19 when he laid the first stone of the "College roial of Oure Lady and Seynt Nicholas" in Cambridge on Passion Sunday, 1441. At the time this marsh town was still a port so, to make way for his college, Henry exercised a form of compulsory purchase and levelled houses, shops, lanes, and wharves, and even a church to make way for his pet project.

PETERBOROUGH CATHEDRAL ▶

A Norman cathedral with an early English west front, a perpendicular retrochoir, a 13th century painted nave ceiling and the tomb of Catherine of Aragon. It was also the former burial place of Mary, Queen of Scots.

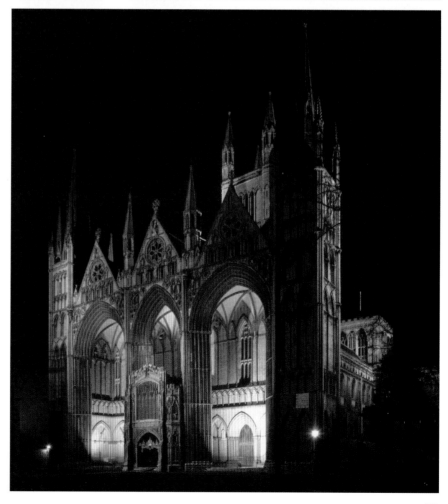

STRATFORD ST. MARY ◀

The church with its pretty tower and clerestory and spectacular flint flushwork is sadly cut off from the village by the main London to Ipswich road which thunders past barely 50 yards away.

BUNGAY BUTTERCROSS ▲

Built in 1689, it replaced the possibly Saxon original that was burnt down in the Great Fire of the previous year.

SOUTHWOLD BEACH HUTS ◀

Looking out over the sand and shingle beach across the North Sea, Southwold beach huts are the essence of old "bucket and spade" holidays.

GREAT YARMOUTH ▼

The *Mayflower* originally set sail for America from nearby Harwich.

THE WASH ▶

This is were King John is supposed to have lost the Crown Jewels in the quickly rising tide. Nobody has found anything, despite all the searching.

U.S. WWII CEMETARY, MADINGLEY ▼

First established December 7, 1943, these 30½ acres, donated by the University of Cambridge, were selected as a permanent American Military Cemetery not only because of the scenic grandeur, but also because a large proportion of American casualties occurred in this general area of East Anglia. The cemetery was dedicated on July 16, 1956.

HEART OF ENGLAND

THE HEART OF ENGLAND ▼

The Heart of England stretches from the coast of Lincolnshire in the east, down to the valleys and hills of Shropshire and Herefordshire, in the west. The land has been cultivated for over 2,000 years and within it lies some of the most stunning countryside anywhere in the British Isles.

HEART OF ENGLAND

One of the best and most relaxing ways to see the area is by taking a boat trip on a traditional barge. A network of navigable waterways makes much of the Heart of England accessible to this peaceful form of transport.

THE COTSWOLDS ▶
Unarguably romantic with country roads leading to peaceful river valleys the Cotswolds are picture-postcard lovely with golden honey-coloured stone villages all set within beautiful green rolling landscapes. Here time really seems to have stood still.

The story of the Heart of England is written in stone—mighty castles, cathedrals, and stately homes; picturesque cottages in sleepy hamlets. The Heart of England stretches from the coast of Lincolnshire in the east, down to the valleys and hills of Shropshire and Herefordshire, in the west. There's 2,000 years of civilisation here in a land famed for its natural beauty. To the north rise the magnificent Derbyshire Dales which are such a marvellous area for walking and observing unspoiled nature. Staffordshire has more miles of canal than any other shire county. Culturally, few locations can match Shakespeare's Stratford-upon-Avon.

Birmingham's pedestrian friendly squares and streets, coupled with venues such as the National Indoor Arena, Symphony Hall, and the NEC Arena attract visitors all year for their various entertainments. Throughout the four boroughs of Wolverhampton, Dudley, Sandwell, and Walsall, there are traditional pubs, excellent restaurants and the warm hospitality and dry sense of humour that Black Country people are renowned for. Amazingly, the last of Wyatt Earp's surviving relatives still live in The Black Country.

Derbyshire contains the country's first national park—the Peak District. With spectacular, unspoilt moorlands and hills, lush valleys, forests, and reservoirs, the Peak District can offer every outdoor pastime. In addition five of the UK's most spectacular show caves are in the Peak District—two of them having the unique Blue John Stone—the only source in the world.

Hardwick Hall in north-east Derbyshire, one of the greatest stately homes of England, has survived since being built during the reign of Elizabeth I. It contains one of Europe's best collections of embroideries and tapestries.

The past meets the future in Leicestershire, from where the very first travel agent, Thomas Cook, organised one of the world's first excursions by train in 1841; however Leicestershire is not stuck in the past, the city of Leicester recently opened the National Space Science Centre.

Oakham, the capital of the tiny county of Rutland, is mentioned in the Domesday Book of 1086. It has a wonderful castle, a fortified Norman manor house.

The lovely county of Shropshire is still very rural and a place where you can really feel that you have stepped back in time. Prime attractions are the Severn Valley Steam Railway, and the shire horses timelessly ploughing at Acton Scott Historic Farm. There's mystery and legend in the hidden

ENGLAND

"shuts" and passages of the medieval county town of Shrewsbury—an area made famous in the Cadfael stories and as the heart of the Industrial Revolution as exemplified by the world's first iron bridge at Coalbrookdale—still a fantastic feat of engineering.

Finally, on no account miss the historic town of Warwick, dominated by its magnificent castle. A magnificent fortress towering over the banks of the River Avon.

SYMONDS YAT ◀
The word *picturesque* was coined to describe Symonds Yat. Tourists have been welcomed to the Wye Gorge since Admiral Nelson visited with his mistress over 200 years ago. Symonds Yat, originally known as Symonds Gate, is a scenic village divided in two by the river. It is great fun to cross the river because the ferryman manually pulls the ferry from one side to the other by means of a rope.

WORCESTERSHIRE WAY ▼
Worcester is home to one of the world's best known sauces, the spicy Worcestershire Sauce, concocted by two chemists in 1835, Lea and Perrins.

BROAD CAMPDEN ▼
The beautiful golden stone of the Cotswolds is shown off well in Broad Campden, Gloucestershire.

MALVERN PRIORY ▶

Great Malvern Priory is dedicated to
Saints Mary and Michael and was
founded in 1085, although the building
standing today is mainly 15th century.
The priory has a collection of stained
glass that is only bettered by York
Minster, it's north transept window
being a gift from King Henry VII.
During World War II all the medieval
glass was removed for safety. When it
was replaced after the war a great deal
of releading and restoration work was
done, leaving the windows in better
condition than for a long time.

LOWER BROCKHAMPTON ▶

This timber-framed building would not
look out of place in Normandy—or
any other medieval location. The Welsh
border counties such as Shropshire,
Herefordshire and Gloucestershire are
well-known for the wealth of unspoilt
historic buildings that have remained—
unlike so many others—untouched by
war since the 17th century.

ANN HATHAWAY'S GARDENS

STRATFORD-UPON-AVON ▶

Stratford-upon-Avon is synonymous
with William Shakespeare. This is the
thatched farmhouse that belonged to
his wife Anne before she married him.
The town has long been a popular
tourist attraction.

ENGLAND

BRINDLEY PLACE BIRMINGHAM ▲
Birmingham has 180 miles of canals
and 216 locks, hence the claim "more
canals than Venice". James Brindley was
a great engineer and canal pioneer.

ALTHORP HOUSE & PARK ◄
Althorp has been the home of the
Spencer family since the early 1500s
when Sir John Spencer acquired the
300-acre estate and built the first house.
This was remodelled in 1786 to the
existing building. An island in the
centre of the lake is the final resting
place of Diana, Princess of Wales.

STRATFORD-UPON-AVON ▶

The Bard's birthplace, his home for many years and also his final resting place, there are five historic houses associated with him and his family in Stratford. It is also home to the Royal Shakespeare Company which has three theatres here. "Strat" is the anglicised form of the Latin *strata* meaning street. It indicates that the place is on or near a Roman road.

ASTON HALL ▶

Aston Hall, Shropshire, was built between 1618 and 1635 for Sir Thomas Holte and is one of the last grand Jacobean houses to be built in England and has survived largely untouched by enthusiastic remodelling from later generations. Aston Hall became a museum and place of public entertainment in 1858.

CHIRK AQUADUCT ▶

The Shropshire Union Canal must be one of the most spectacular and scenic canals in Britain. The Chirk aquaduct has 10 arches and is 70ft high and 600ft long. It carries the Welsh Canal over the River Ceiriog at Chirk. It was designed by Thomas Telford and opened in 1801. A railroad viaduct runs alongside.

ENGLAND

WARWICK CASTLE ▶ ▼

Raised on a small escarpment above the River Avon
Warwick castle dominates its environs and has been
home to the Earls of Warwick for generations. Most of
the exterior dates from the mid-14th century although
the castle inevitably has been much changed over the
years. In the early 1700s a Jacobean wing was added. It
contains an impressive collection of armoury, paintings,
and treasures, many of which were collected during the
18th century fashion for grand tours of the Continent.

BELVOIR CASTLE ▶

Belvoir Castle commands a magnificent view of the Vale of Belvoir. The name Belvoir meaning "beautiful view" dates back to Norman times when Robert de Toden built the first castle on the site; destruction caused by two civil wars and a fire in 1816 have breached the continuity of Belvoir's history.

BIDDULPH GRANGE GARDEN ▲

A rare and exciting survival of a High Victorian garden which contains elaborate ornamentation, Biddulph has recently been restored by the National Trust. The garden is divided into a series of themed gardens, with a Chinese temple, Egyptian court, dahlia walk, glen, and many other settings.

CHATSWORTH HOUSE ▼

The original house was built for Bess of Hardwick in the 1550s but it was rebuilt by 1707 with a new classic facade. "Capability" Brown landscaped the grounds a century later when he cleared away the formal gardens. Over time the house has been extensively altered and enlarged as have the gardens. The arboretum, the pinetum, and rock gardens were created by Joseph Paxton, later the creator of the Crystal Palace for the Great Exhibition, but also one of the great names in garden history. Inside the house are fine collections of furniture, paintings, drawings, and books.

ENGLAND

RIVER DERWENT ▲
Today the Ladybower, Derwent, and Howden reservoirs are surrounded by woodland and lakeside walks. The River Derwent was extensively used until 1795 when the Derby Canal opened.

SHERWOOD FOREST
NOTTINGHAMSHIRE ◄
Ancient Sherwood Forest has some 450 acres, but at the time of Domesday it covered most of Nottinghamshire above the River Trent. The Major Oak in which Robin Hood and his men hid is still there to be seen.

BURGHLEY HOUSE ▶

Built by William Cecil in 1587 and occupied by his descendants ever since, inside are 18 treasure-filled state rooms. The treasures include art collections, wood carvings, silver-decorated fireplaces, and magnificent ceilings painted by Verrio.

WEST STOCKWITH,

CHESTERFIELD CANAL ▼

This 17th century watermill contains a permanent exhibition of the possessions and works of the poet, Alfred Lord Tennyson.

YORKSHIRE

YORKSHIRE DALES ▼

The gigantic sweep of the Yorkshire Dales fold in great ridges over the countryside. Water rushes down the sides of these steep hills to form the many rivers—the Swale, Ure, Nidd, Wharfe, Aire, and Calder—all of which flow through the Dales to meet the River Ouse around the city of York; this then feeds into the River Humber and thence out to the North Sea.

YORKSHIRE

For more than 2,000 years Yorkshire has dared to be different. England's biggest county has never lost a sense of being special. Yorkshire has a grandeur you don't get anywhere else, the power of its history and pride of its people make this a place where "ordinary" simply won't do. The county actually feels big with its spreading high moorlands and impressive dales. English history has always revolved around who controls Yorkshire, it has always been economically important and strategically crucial.

Yorkshire really is sublimely beautiful. There are more ruined abbeys and castles, great houses and gardens here than anywhere else. In addition, the landscape contributes magnificent high moors, wooded hills, and lush farming country. Three National Parks—the Yorkshire Dales, the Peak District, and the North York Moors—protect more than 1,000 square miles of matchless walking country.

Yorkshire's grandeur is inspirational. The Brontës of Haworth, sculptor Henry Moore, the late Poet Laureate Ted Hughes, artist David Hockney, composer Delius, superb choirs and the world best brass bands—all came from Yorkshire.

There are two World Heritage Sites in the county, the latest the great wool mill complex of Saltaire on the edge of Bradford, and Studley Royal Park which includes the romantic ruins of Fountains Abbey.

Yorkshire also has a long North Sea coast-line with miles of golden beaches, majestic cliffs, and great seaside resorts. Scarborough, Bridlington, and Cleethorpes bustle with life,

YORKSHIRE COUNTRYSIDE ▲
Moorland meets farming country.

while Filey and Hornsea are traditional favourites. Yorkshire vision changed the world. Captain Cook learned his skills at the historic port of Whitby and sailed round the world in a flat-bottomed Yorkshire collier boat. William Wilberforce left Hull to abolish slavery. The South Pennines were the birth-place of the Industrial Revolution and the might of Yorkshire industry made Britain a world power.

Up in the north of Yorkshire sits the beautiful city of York. In its time it has been

a Roman stronghold and Viking capital, and is still one of Europe's greatest medieval cities. York Minster is the largest Gothic cathedral in northern Europe and domi-nates the city. The Foundations Museum under the Minster shows how the present building was constructed on the site of a Norman cathedral, which was itself built on a Roman fort. There are many museums and galleries in the city which explain York's impressive history. One of the best is The Jorvik Viking Centre which breathes fresh life into York's Viking past in a brand new interpretation of 10th century Jorvik. Deep beneath the pavements of modern-day York, the Viking-age city has been constructed in incredible detail following recent research into archaeological evidence found on this site.

Yorkshire is so full of magnificent buildings that it is almost invidious to name any without mentioning them all. However, mention must be made of Castle Howard, the largest and most spectacular stately home in Yorkshire which has been loved and cared for by succeeding generations of the Howard family since the 18th century. Furthermore, it has always been open to the public.

Near Leeds lies another magnificent building—Harewood House. Designed by John Carr and completed in 1772 for Edwin Lascelles, Harewood House has been lived in by his family ever since. The mag-nificent interior, created by Robert Adam, has superb ceilings and plasterwork and contains what the best collection of Chippendale furniture anywhere.

CONISBROUGH CASTLE ▶

The ruins here belong to a Norman
stronghold built originally in wood,
probably on top of Saxon defences.
Although later built of stone it had
already badly decayed by Tudor times.
Sir Walter Scott loved Conisbrough and
used the tiny third floor chapel as the
setting for a scene in his great romantic
novel *Ivanhoe*.

MIDDLEHAM CASTLE ▶

Although the castle was much
dismantled in 1646, significant remains
include the keep built in the 1170s,
with walls standing to nearly their original height, the banqueting hall, a 13th
century chapel, 14th century gatehouse,
and deep moat. Richard III acquired
the castle in 1471 and his son was born
here. A replica of the famous
Middleham Jewel is on display.

CASTLE HOWARD ▶

Castle Howard is the magnificent 18th
century home of the Howard family. It
was designed by John Vanbrugh and
built with rose and cream stone. The
central dramatic feature which makes
Castle Howard so instantly recognisable
is the huge central dome. Known
worldwide as "Brideshead" from the
television series *Brideshead Revisited*, it
also featured as "Longlands" in the TV
series *The Buccaneers*.

ENGLAND

RICHMOND CASTLE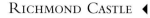

One of the most imposing Norman remains in England towers beside the River Swale near the town of Richmond in North Yorkshire. It was built between c.1080 and 1170. The curtain walls, which are up to 10ft thick in places, was built in the 1080s by Alan the Red. The 12th century rectangular keep was once 100ft high and one of the finest in the country.

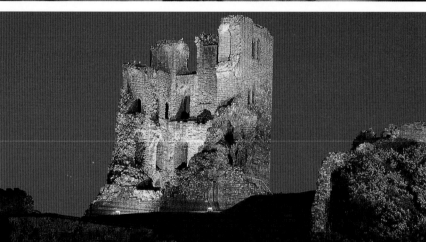

SCARBOROUGH CASTLE

Scarborough Castle is sited on the remains of a 4th century Roman signal station on a headland above the town. The castle itself dates from the original 12th century castle incorporating the substantial remains of a great rectangular keep.

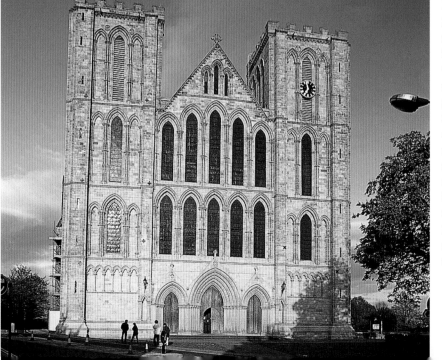

RIPON CATHEDRAL ◀

Ripon Cathedral, although relatively small for its importance, is notable for its superb Early English 13th century west front, 14th century stained glass, and 15th century wood carvings. It was greatly restored in the 19th century. In fact until 1836 this was only a parish church although its twin towers are reminiscent of Norman cathedral design. Lying below the central tower, the crypt is all that remains of the original church of St Wilfrid. It is believed to be the oldest complete crypt in Europe (excluding Italy). Dating from 672AD. The crypt is also one of the earliest Christian shrines in England.

SELBY ABBEY ▶

Selby Abbey has foundations dating back to 1069 and is composed of a combination of late Norman and Early English styles. It is a magnificent example of a monastic abbey finding a new purpose as a parish church and is probably the most outstanding of its kind in the north of England.

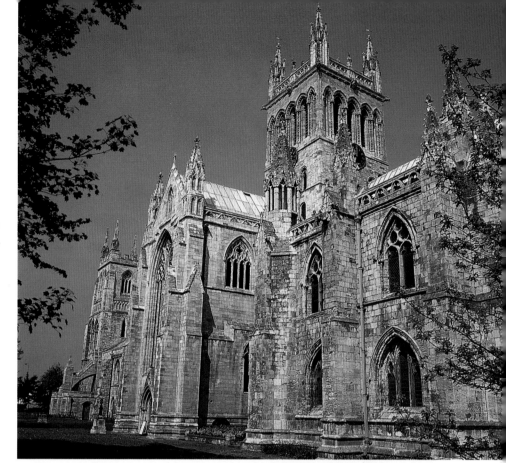

BEVERLEY MINSTER ▶

Medieval Gothic architecture in the English Perpendicular style the Church of St John the Evangelist, Beverley Minster is on the site of a Saxon church and is the most splendid collegiate church in the country. Beneath the high altar lies a holy well, a reminder of earlier pagan times. The Percy tomb is the burial place of St John of Beverley, and is a masterpiece of Decorated design. Also of note are a Saxon sanctuary chair, and a large collection of fine misericord seats dating from 1520.

RIEVAULX ABBEY ▶

Founded by 12 Cistercians in 1131 in a remote part of the Rye Valley in North Yorkshire, the ruins of this beautiful abbey are some of the most romantic anywhere in the world. The abbey rapidly grew grander and bigger after its foundation and by around 1150 was home to 140 monks and 500 lay brothers. The abbey was largely destroyed in 1539 during the Dissolution of the Monasteries by Henry VIII.

ENGLAND

BENINGBROUGH HALL ◀

This handsome Queen Anne house was built in 1716. The Hall contains 100 portraits of the period 1688-1760 on loan from the National Portrait Gallery, and a Victorian laundry showing 19th century domestic life. Outside the walled garden has been restored, there is a wilderness area, childrens' playground, and potting shed.

BRONTË PARSONAGE ◀

The house in Haworth was built in 1778 and now belongs to the Brontë Society. The Brontës were an extraordinary family, Charlotte, Emily, and Anne wrote some of the greatest novels in the English language, including *Jane Eyre*, *Wuthering Heights* and *The Tenant of Wildfell Hall*. Haworth Parsonage was their lifelong home, while its moorland setting provided them with constant inspiration.

HAREWOOD HOUSE, ◀

Designed by John Carr in 1759 for Edwin Lascelles, Harewood House in Leeds has been lived in by his family ever since. A variety of paintings are displayed, including Italian Renaissance works, Turner, Reynolds, Gainsborough, Girtin, plus 18th century portraits and 20th century masterpieces. The house was built between 1759 and 1771 to the designs of John Carr of York. In 1772 "Capability" Brown started work on the surrounding park.

OAKWELL HALL ▶

This moated manor house in Birstall was the family home to Civil War Royalists. Teeming with memories and images of the past, Oakwell Hall still contains its 17th century decoration and oak furniture. The Hall was an inspiration to Charlotte Brontë who featured as a setting in her novel *Shirley*.

SHIBDEN HALL ▶

Shibden Hall in Halifax dates originally from around 1420. It is a distinctive half-timbered house with later additions. It has period rooms furnished in the styles of the 17th, 18th, and 19th century. An important barn houses the West Yorkshire Folk Museum which contains a collection of horse-drawn vehicles and old agricultural implements. The hall was once the home of the noted 19th century diarist Anne Lister.

VICTORIA CENTRE & GARDENS

HARROGATE ▶

Harrogate has all the old-fashioned dignity of a popular spa town and has long been a favourite place for "taking the waters". The sulphury mineral springs were discovered in 1571 but the first public baths did not appear until 1842 with the Royal Pump Room. Genteel crowds came to Harrogate in the 18th and especially 19th century.

ENGLAND

THE ROYAL ARMOURIES MUSEUM ▲

The Royal Armouries in Leeds houses 3,000 years of military history through over 8,000 spectacular exhibits. The stunning surroundings make this world famous collection of arms and armour a must-see attraction for anyone interested in warfare.

HUMBER BRIDGE & HUMBER BRIDGE COUNTRY PARK ▲

The park contains the restored remains of an old mill (not working), a picnic area, woodlands, meadows, and wetlands. The Humber Bridge is nearby.

LAKE GORMIRE ▼

Gormire is a tranquil tarn-like lake which provides a breeding place for coot, great crested grebe, and mallard.

Viaduct on the River Nidd ▶

Knaresborough is a good starting point for tours of the Dales. It sits on a bluff above the River Nidd and has the ruins of a castle above the town.

Runswick Bay ▼

Runswick Bay is a picture-postcard sea-side village much loved by both artists and holidaymakers alike.

Thornwick Bay ▶

Flamborough Head is a rocky chalk headland jutting out into the sea which rises from grassy chalk wolds. At its feet lie picturesque coves and numerous sea caves. The sea itself is dangerous for shipping here and many ships have foundered here. In 1779 people stood on the head to watch John Paul Jones beat two English men-o-wars out at sea.

NORTH-WEST

NORTH-WEST

England's north-west encompasses the counties of Lancashire, Cheshire, Greater Manchester, and Merseyside. It is a region of vibrant cities, seaside resorts, and breathtaking countryside. It also contains the very centre of the United Kingdom—in 1991, Dunsop Bridge was officially recognised as such by the Ordnance Survey. BT marked it by placing its 100,000th telephone box on the village green.

The north-west contains some of Britain's most unspoilt countryside, such as the Ribble Valley, in which sit picture postcard villages, bubbling brooks, and hump-back stone bridges, all set against a panoramic backdrop of majestic hillsides. A microcosm of England at her glorious best, this green and verdant land is still one of the nation's best kept secrets. Time stands still in ancient villages where little seems to have changed over the centuries. This is Lancashire witch country and Pendle Hill looms large over spellbinding historic hamlets such as Sabden, Newchurch, Downham, and Barley.

The rivers Ribble, Hodder, and Calder wind freely through the rich pastures, where contented sheep graze alongside riverbanks that the Romans once trod. Clitheroe and its Norman castle and keep dominate the limestone rock high above the town's main thoroughfares, forming an impressive backdrop. In the villages, little has changed over the centuries. Downham is a rural idyll: even television aerials are banned.

Cheshire is a special place. Its location, on the border with Wales and at the meeting point of the Midlands and England's rugged North Country, has led to a rich and eventful history set within a melting pot of landscapes. Here outdoor enthusiasts are rewarded with intimate glimpses of peaceful English countryside, ranging from magical wooded hillsides and gentle pastoral lowlands, to the panoramic heights of purple moorland and wild hills. The Sandstone and Gritstone Trails are two spectacular, contrasting routes with fine views over the surrounding countryside.

The two biggest cities in the area are Manchester and Liverpool. Manchester mixes the best of the old with the best of the new. Sleek contemporary buildings merge with Victorian architecture: take the Lowry—housing a large collection of the artist's "matchstick men" paintings—rises from the regenerated docklands at Salford Quays. A constellation of superb 19th century public buildings and churches sit within a city which is mad about sport—particularly football—shopping, and socialising.

Over on the west coast lies Liverpool, one of the main ports of embarkation for the New World. For millions of people all over the world, however, Liverpool means the Beatles. Perhaps because it is so close to the sea, there is something magical about the evening sky in Liverpool, which throws a beautiful light on the grand architecture and creates gorgeous silhouettes of the famous Liver Birds. It's a wonderful place to go to the theatre, the opera or to wander along the famous waterfront at the Albert Dock.

MANCHESTER G-MEX ▶

From a windmill in 1812 to today's state-of-the-art exhibition and international convention centre in the heart of Manchester.

LANCASTER CANAL ▼

During the late 18th century the industrial demand for transport between Manchester, Preston, Lancaster, and Kendal gave rise to proposals to build a broad beam canal from Westhoughton, east of Wigan, and Kendal. A surveyor named John Rennie produced a proposal that included several aqueducts and eight locks near the Kendal end at Tewitfield. Based on this survey, construction began in 1792.

BEACH AT BLACKPOOL ◀

Blackpool beach has been a popular holiday centre for over a century.

ENGLAND

CHOLMONDELEY CASTLE ▲

Cholmondeley Castle garden is said by many to be among the most romantically beautiful gardens they have ever seen. Even the wild orchids, daisies, and buttercups take on an aura of glamour in this beautifully landscaped setting.

PORT OF LIVERPOOL BUILDING ▲

The Port of Liverpool Building was constructed in 1907, and is distinguished by its beautiful copper dome. It has black and gilded globes on the gate posts and several figures of King Neptune on the ornamented pillars at intervals along the stone balustrade.

TATTON PARK ◄

Now owned by the National Trust, Tatton Park, Cheshire was started in the early 19th century for William Egerton. The deer park covers 1,000 acres. The gardens include an authentic Japanese garden and an Italian garden, plus 54 acres landscaped by Humphrey Repton into formal gardens and woodlands with lakes, tree-lined avenues, and herds of red and fallow deer. The house contains an impressive collection of paintings,—including works by Canaletto, van Dyck, Murillo, and Chardin—books, silver, glass, china, and furniture.

SADDLEWORTH MOOR ▶

Saddleworth is the general name for the string of settlements in the Tame valley and the moorland area beyond. From the 18th century onwards it became an important textile-manufacturing area and contains many relics of the Industrial Revolution: old farmhouses, 18th century weavers' cottages, mills, the Huddersfield Narrow Canal, and an impressive railway viaduct.

FOXDENTON HALL ▶

The Foxdenton heritage started in the early 1400s when Elizabeth Radcliffe married her cousin Robert Radcliffe and they built the first Foxdenton Hall as their home. William Radcliffe, the "Foxdenton Redhead," rebuilt the Hall in 1620. He was killed together with his son and heir, Robert, fighting for at the Battle of Edgehill in 1642, and it was Alexander (Radclyffe) who was responsible for rebuilding the hall in 1700 as it is seen today. The last of the Radclyffes was Charles Robert Eustace who died in 1953 thus bringing to an end the long line of Radclyffes, who had lived and loved Foxdenton Hall.

CHESTER CATHEDRAL AT NIGHT ▲
The cathedral was founded as a
Benedictine Monastery and dedicated
to St Werburgh in 1092. However, there
are records of a church on this site since
the early 10th century.

BRAMALL HALL ◀
Situated in Cheshire, Bramall Hall is
one of the county's grandest black and
white timber-framed buildings. The
oldest parts of Bramall date from the
14th century, however, the manor has
been held in other forms since the time
of the Saxons.

BELMONT ◀
Belmont enjoys a rich tradition of
textile finishing, cotton dyeing, and
cotton bleaching, a trade that spans the
last 200 years.

SMITHILLS HALL, BOLTON ▶

One of the oldest manor houses in Lancashire, with parts dating from the 14th century, although there are more recent additions such as the great hall built in the 15th century with a fine exposed timber roof. In 1554 George Marsh was questioned here during his trial, it is said that a mark on a flagstone inside the building was made when he stamped his foot in fury.

LUNE AQUEDUCT LANCASHIRE ▶

Opened in 1797, the aqueduct carries the Kendal to Preston canal over the River Lune. The architect was John Rennie and his engineer was Alexander Stephens. The aqueduct is regarded as one of the finest examples of canal engineering in the country, combining enormous strength with great elegance.

LANCASTER GATE ▶

This is one of the best preserved castles in the country. A Roman fort with a garrison of 500 horsemen once stood on the site of the present castle. The first fortifications were built during early Norman times, with the great square keep built c 1170. Other additions and improvements were made over the centuries. The castle was a Parliamentary stronghold during the Civil War and in more recent times it has been used as the jail for assize and other courts.

NORTHUMBRIA

KIELDER WATER ▼

The Kielder Water Bird of Prey Centre is located within the magnificent forest and lakeside surroundings of Kielder Water, Northumberland at Leaplish Waterside Park. The water is over seven miles long and covers 2,684 acres. Kielder is the largest forest in England at 200 square miles and is also one of the largest man-made forests in Europe. The area is named after the village of Kielder and comes from the Old Norse *kelda* meaning spring.

NORTHUMBRIA

The ancient kingdom of Northumbria, today covering the four northerly areas of Durham, Northumberland, the Tees Valley, and Tyne and Wear, is especially rich in historic remains. Over this land battles have been fought, castles built, and legends written—stirring tales of battles and bishops, saints and centurions. Numerous historic houses, gardens, and museums are set against a backdrop of glorious countryside and incomparable coastline.

Northumbria has always been the battleground between the English and Scots, border country as the huge stone castles make very plain—those at Alnwick and Bamburgh have to be seen to be believed. As well as these there are two World Heritage Sites at Hadrian's Wall and Durham, two national parks, and the beginnings of Christianity on Holy Island.

Indeed, the ancient region of Northumbria is blessed with a wealth of Christian cultural heritage, going back to AD635, when St Aidan carried the Christian message to Northumbria from Iona. He settled on the Holy Island of Lindisfarne, where he founded a monastery. The story of the Christian mission that followed was described by the first English historian, the Venerable Bede. More can be discovered about the great scholar, his life and times, by visiting Bede's World in Jarrow. Lindisfarne is also remembered for St Cuthbert, the shepherd boy who reluctantly became a bishop.

Many years later, Viking raids prompted the monks of Lindisfarne to flee, carrying with them the treasured relics of this popu-

ANGEL OF THE NORTH ▲
Steel sculpture by Antony Gormley.

TYNE BRIDGE AT SUNSET ▶ ▲

WARKWORTH CASTLE ▶
Warkworth made such an impression on William Shakespeare that he used this splendid 12th century castle as a setting for Henry IV.

lar saint, eventually laying his bones to rest in Durham in AD995. Durham Cathedral is a masterpiece of Romanesque architecture, and has become a World Heritage Site. It also contains the shrines of the Venerable Bede and St Cuthbert which continue to attract pilgrims to this day.

Northumbria is renowned for its countryside—Pennine moors and dales, river valleys and coastline from the ramparts and beaches of Berwick to the broad sands at Saltburn. Long stretches of the Northumberland coast have been designated areas of outstanding natural beauty. Here you can explore fishing villages with working harbours, visit traditional seaside towns, and discover the region's colourful maritime heritage—such as at Hartlepool Historic Quay where you can visit HMS *Trincomalee*, the world's oldest floating warship. The great explorer Captain Cook is a son of this region, and his birthplace museum can be found in nearby Middlesbrough.

The Northumbrian coast has quiet fishing communities like Craster, known for its oak-smoked kippers, and Bamburgh, famed for its rocky fortress and sea heroine Grace Darling who rescued drowning sailors. Seahouses, a busy little traditional seaside town, is the embarkation point for sea trips to the Farne Islands. North Shields, on the river Tyne, is the region's busiest fishing harbour.

Powerful families also once ruled Northumbria, building impressive fortified homes—Barnard Castle was a Norman stronghold; Raby Castle the home of the Neville family, that governed large tracts of County Durham; Dunstanburgh was the property of the Duke of Lancaster; and Alnwick Castle has always been the home of the Percys, Dukes of Northumberland.

The biggest city in the region is Newcastle-upon-Tyne, sited strategically at the east end of Hadrian's Wall. A number of impressive bridges cross the river here, but easily the most distinctive is the Tyne Bridge built in 1928 which dominates the city.

DUNSTANBURGH CASTLE ▼

Badly damaged during the Wars of the Roses these romantic ruins occupy about nine acres of dramatic coastline on top of 100ft cliffs. This extensive 14th century castle is the largest in Northumberland. It is reached only by a gentle 1.5-mile walk from Craster or Embleton.

ALNWICK CASTLE ▲

A magnificent border fortress dating back to the 11th century, Alnwick was much adapted and extended over the centuries until it was extensively restored by Robert Adam in the mid-19th century. William the Lion, King of Scotland was captured here during an attempt to besiege the castle in 1174.

BAMBURGH CASTLE ◀

This stunning coastal site has been occupied with a fortress since the Iron Age; indeed, Angle kings once ruled Northumbria from here. The present 11th century castle was a Norman stronghold which survived many sieges and welcomed many English kings as guests. During the Wars of the Roses it was held by the Lancastrians and was twice besieged. However, on the second occasion Bamburgh became the first castle in England to succumb to gunfire when the walls fell to the pounding artillery directed by Richard Neville, Earl of Warwick (the Kingmaker).

Lindisfarne, Holy Island ▶

Built on the orders of Henry VIII in 1550 (using stones taken from Lindisfarne Priory) to protect Holy Island from attack by the Scots, the castle was converted into a magnificent private home by the architect Sir Edwin Lutyens in 1903. The island is now a wildlife sanctuary.

Tynemouth Castle ▶

The castle dates from 7th century and is the burial place of the kings of Northumbria. The ruins date from the 11th and 14th century. The priory was destroyed by the Danes in 865 but was refounded as a Benedictine Priory. It was fortified later, but is now a picturesque ruin.

Beadnell Bay ▼

Low Dover is virtually encompassed by the sea, being situated at the end of a tiny peninsula on the Northumbria Coast at Beadnell. It has wonderful sandy beaches and safe yachting in the wide bay.

COLLEGE VALLEY ▼
A view of Auchope Cairn and Cheviot Summit looking down College Valley.

BOWES MUSEUM ▲
A famous feature of the Bowes Museum in Barnard Castle is a life-size mechanical swan which periodically catches a mechanical fish. Also on display is a remarkable 18th century French decorative art collection and magnificent paintings by El Greco, Goya, Canaletto, Courbet, Boucher, and Tiepolo.

DURHAM CATHEDRAL ◀
Built in the late 11th and early 12th centuries to house the relics of St Cuthbert, the evangelist of Northumbria, and the Venerable Bede, the cathedral attests to the importance of the early Benedictine monastic community and is the largest and best example of Norman-style architecture in England.

SUNDERLAND WINTER GARDENS ▶
Overlooking the North Terrace of Mowbray Park and connecting to the Museum and Art Gallery, the spectacular Winter Gardens offer a world of lush tropical plants, exotic blooms, and amazing water features. The Winter Gardens were opened in 1879.

ALNMOUTH ▶
At the mouth of the River Aln—which for centuries has provided a natural sheltered anchorage for both fishermen and seaborne travellers—it is probable that there once existed a community who would have been among the earliest in the district to receive Christianity. It would have been brought to them by the missionaries of Iona who had been sent for by Oswald, King of Northumberland, in about the year 634. He wanted the missionaries to help him to persuade his people to accept this new religion and forsake their old pagan customs.

NEW TYNE BRIDGE ▶
Although the Tyne Bridge is the most famous of the six bridges that cross between Newcastle and Gateshead, it was only finished in 1928 (when it was the largest single span bridge in the world). The hydraulically-operated swivel mechanism allowed taller fixed-mast vessels to reach further upstream than before. The Swing Bridge was built by Lord Armstrong and opened in 1876. It crosses at about the same point as the Roman and medieval bridges. The High Level bridge for rail and road traffic was built in 1849 by Robert Stephenson.

CUMBRIA

The Lake District is possibly the most beautiful place in Britain, contrasting the lush green of the valleys and lakesides with the harshness of stone crags and fells. Wonderful at any time of year, each season brings different colours and hues that inspire walkers and climbers, artists and poets.

CUMBRIA

Cumbria possesses a rich and colourful history, including the notable figures of the Emperor Hadrian, Rob Roy, and William Wordsworth. Like Northumbria Cumbria borders Scotland and was a battlefield between the two lands—particularly Carlisle, that blends its unique heritage with the modern-day facilities of a traffic-free city centre. The great border city stands proudly at the gateway to one of the most fascinating areas of our country. Here you can see and touch Roman finds and replicas, discover all about the turbulent history of the notorious Border Reivers, or explore the mighty castle and picturesque cathedral.

Cumbria's greatest jewel is the Lake District, whose lakes are familiar to all poetry and literature lovers—Windermere offers all manner of lake activities, as does Coniston Water, with the "Old Man" (2,634ft) towering above. Thirlmere provides clear and pure contemplation, while Ullswater is popular for sailing.

Nowhere else will you find nature and culture in such close proximity. Grasmere has Dove Cottage, with Rydal Mount Close nearby, both former homes of Wordsworth. Sawrey is where Beatrix Potter's animal characters sprang to life. At Grizedale Forest, you'll find a fascinating sculpture trail, whilst Brantwood, John Ruskin's home above Coniston Water, offers an insight into the life of this influential writer.

The local towns are equally as evocative —from historic Kendal, famous for its mint cake and castle, to Bowness-on-Windermere from where pleasure craft ply the lake all year round. Keswick-on-Derwentwater is a focal point for the northern half of the National Park, boasting the mighty Skiddaw (3,054ft) as a backdrop. The Borrowdale Valley, so enticing to serious walkers and climbers, leads to Lodore Falls and the Honiter Pass, an area of wildly contrasting countryside, taking in the sheltered Eden Valley, beautiful Northern Lakes and spectacular open moor-

land of the north Pennines. Unspoilt by industry and untouched by visitors Eden offers a rural retreat for anyone looking for a peace away from the hustle and bustle of daily life.

Cumbria is not just about countryside: the towns are well worth a visit. At Appleby you can relax by the wonderful riverside setting; Penrith is a peaceful country town containing an ancient castle, interesting alleyways, and a traditional market; and Keswick retains the attractive appearance of a traditional small market town, the weekly stalls still set around the Moot (market) hall which dominates the town centre.

But in the end it is the lakes and fells that bring in the visitors—steep-sided glacial valleys which cut deeply into the central part of the Lake District such as Borrowdale and Buttermere; to the north, east, and west the softer and more open outlines make a striking contrast with impressive views. Derwentwater, Buttermere, and Crummock Water, Bassenthwaite Lake, and Thirlmere all have their own individual characteristics, but share in peacefulness and accessibility.

To the east, on the Cartmel Peninsula, lies Grange-over-sands, an Edwardian seaside resort with ornamental gardens and guided walks across the sands. The market town of Ulverston marks the gateway to the Furness Peninsula and has many claims to fame, including the world's only Laurel and Hardy Museum. There is also an opportunity to watch glass blowing or visit the colourful sweet market, every Thursday and Saturday.

HARDKNOTT ◀

Along the line of Hadrian's Wall there were 16 forts, not counting temporary encampments used as overnight camps (marching forts) or as bases for the building of roads, permanent forts and the wall itself.

WRAY CASTLE ▶

This is not a real castle but rather a private house built in in the Gothic Revival Style in 1840 by the architect, H. P. Horner. It was built for Dr Dawson, a retired Liverpool surgeon, and is now owned by the National Trust. The house was built using his wife's inheritance made from a gin distilling fortune. The story goes that she took one look at the house when it was finished, and refused to live in it.

SIZERGH CASTLE ▶

Standing in 1,556 acres, this is one of the best houses in Cumbria. Sizergh Castle has been in the care of the National Trust since 1950, but was formerly occupied by the Strickland family for 730 years. Originally built around 1239 and 1340 as a peel tower by Sir Walter Strickland, it received many additions and improvements over the next 400 years or so. A wing was added to the tower in either the 14th or 15th century, then another two wings in the 16th century.

KIRKSTONE PASS ▶

Kirkstone Pass is the longest and highest road in the Lake District at 1,476 feet above sea level. The pass links Ullswater and Penrith to Windermere. Welcome refreshment is offered at the Kirkstone Pass Inn at the top.

ENGLAND

Castle Appleby ▲
Ranulph le Meschin probably began building Appleby Castle around 1100, passing it to the Crown when le Meschin was made Earl of Chester in 1121. The Scottish king William the Lion took the castle in 1136 without a fight and it was not regained until 1157.

St Bees Cliff ▼
The small resort of St Bees has a 12th century church, jointly dedicated to St Mary and St Bega, it is all that remains of a Benedictine priory founded in the reign of Henry I. The church has been restored and altered in the 19th century.

Wordsworth House ▲
Cockermouth, northern gateway to the lakes, is perhaps best known as the birthplace of William Wordsworth in 1770, one of the most famous poets England has produced. Wordsworth House was built in 1745 and is now owned by the National Trust.

Ravenglass Eskdale Railway ▼
This 15in narrow gauge railroad carries passengers from the old Roman Port of Ravenglass seven miles along the Eskdale Valley to Eskdale (Dalegarth) with a journey time of 40 minutes from Ravenglass to Eskdale.

CUMBRIA

EAMONT BRIDGE ▲

A battle was fought here between the retreating Jacobite army of "Bonnie" Prince Charlie in the 1745 Rebellion and the pursuing English forces. Nearby lies King Arthur's Round Table, a prehistoric earthwork, with Mayburgh Henge another half a mile to the west, both are ancient sites of interest.

BLEA TARN ▼

Blea Tarn is one of the easiest tarns to visit and contains brown trout, perch, and pike. It has a wonderful backdrop of the Langdale Pikes, being at the very heart of wild Lakeland. Rhododendrons on the rocky west shore add to the charm.

CASTLERIGG ▲

Castlerigg Stone Circle is one of the most visually impressive prehistoric monuments in Britain. It is about 100ft in diameter and formed of 38 megalithic stones with another 10 stones forming an inner feature. The stone circle is on the level top of a low hill with magnificent views across to Skiddaw, Blencathra, and Lonscale Fell.

LAKE WINDERMERE ▼

Beautifully situated on the shores of Lake Windermere, the largest lake in England, Low Wood commands spectacular views across the lake to the magnificent Langdale Pikes.

ENGLAND

BASSENTHWAITE ◀ ▲
Bassenthwaite Lake, owned by the National Park Authority, is one of the largest at 4 miles long and ¾ mile wide, however, it also one of the shallowest at only 70ft at its deepest.

SILVER HOW ▲
View towards Grasmere from Silver How.

GRASMERE ◀
Grasmere is famed for Dove Cottage, the home of William Wordsworth and his sister Dorothy.

DERWENTWATER ◀
Keswick is the chief town of the North Lake District and is beautifully situated near the north shore of Lake Derwentwater between the towering hills of Skiddaw and Saddleback. The town is built using local gray stone with narrow streets and old buildings. This is a place much beloved by poets, writers, and artists, including Wordsworth, Coleridge, Shelley, Lamb, Scott, Ruskin, Tennyson, and Robert Louis Stevenson, to name but a few. This view shows the southend of the lake.

LOUGHRIGG ▶

This is a tarn of outstanding beauty—being almost circular in form, with striking views north-west towards the Langdale Pikes, and with a variety of aquatic plants around its margins. Wordsworth described it as being a "most beautiful example" of a lake.

WASTWATER, CUMBRIA ▶

Wastwater is about three miles long and the deepest lake in England, reaching nearly 260ft in places. On one side lie the Screes, a forbidding wall of rubble and all around lie challenging mountains making it a great place for strenuous walking.

CAT BELLS ▼

Not far from Keswick, above the western shore of Derwentwater Lake lies Cat Bells. From here there are good views in all directions from the summit. This area is gentler for walking than other nearby routes.

ENGLAND

GREAT GABLE ◀ ▲
The north and south sides of Great Gable are very precipitous but other routes to the 2,949ft summit are possible, although it calls for some hard walking, but worth the effort because the views are tremendous. This is one of the most popular of the Lake District Fells so you will never feel lonely.

SKIDDAW ▲
Dominating the northern skyline of Keswick, Skiddaw is one of the highest of the Fells in the Lake District at 3,054ft. The peak offers some of the best views over the town and south over Derwentwater Lake towards Helvellyn and Borrowdale, and Bassenthwaite Lake to its west. The north side slopes down through Uldale Fells.

HELVELLYN ◀
There are great views to be seen from the top of this famous Fell, one of the highest in the Lake District at 3,118ft high. Nearby is Striding Edge, also very popular with walkers. Many famous visitors have made this demanding climb including William Wordsworth and Sir Walter Scott.

SIDE PIKE ▶

When traversing around Side Pike, the narrow path passes between the main face of the crag and a large boulder, which is quite a squeeze to get through, especially with a rucksack.

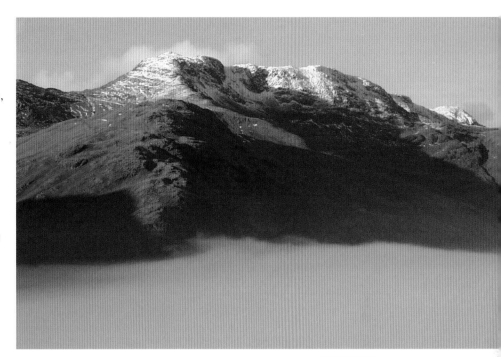

THE OLD MAN ▼

The Old Man of Coniston (2,633ft) rises dramatically behind the houses when seen from the village. Coniston is a good centre for walkers and climbers, and those wanting to investigate the Tilberthwaite Slate quarries. The Coniston Fells run along the north-west side of Coniston Water which is 5½ miles long.

WALES

WELSH COAST ▼

Surely one of the most beautiful coastlines in the temperate world, Wales has perfect sandy beaches as well as rocky splendour. From the Gower Peninsula, the sandy inlets of Pembrokeshire, past Portmeirion and Anglesey, and one to the wild north, the Welsh coast is a joy to visit.

WALES

Clwyd—Wales—is a land of mountains and valleys, and so much more. It is very different in character between north and south, mountain and coast, town and country. The ancient heritage of Wales is apparent all over the country in the form of its language, buildings, tombs and ancient monuments. Wales is rich in legends and stories that perpetuate the folk laws and traditions of this magical land.

One of the great demarcations between Wales and England is Offa's Dyke. Built by Offa, the King of Mercia in the eighth century, it is a giant earthwork in the form of a bank and ditch

running almost complete from Prestatyn on the North Wales coast, to Wye in the south. The Dyke marked out the continually disputed border between Celtic Wales and Saxon Mercia. There is now a tough but walkable pathway for 177 miles beside the Dyke, established by the Countryside Commission in 1971.

South Wales is the most populous part of the country; the famous Welsh Valleys are here and it was here that the Industrial Revolution brought prosperity and people looking for work. Just before World War 2 over half the population of Wales lived in Glamorgan. Two important cities sit on the coast, Cardiff at the

mouth of the River Severn and Swansea further west on the Bristol Channel. The former is the capital of Wales and sits at the estuaries of the rivers Rhymney, Taff and Ely. There was already a settlement here when the Romans made Cardiff an important town and built a castle, and Cardiff has grown over the centuries into an important political and cultural centre.

Swansea sits at the base of the Gower peninsula and was possibly founded by the Vikings. It became a big industrial city in the 19th century exporting iron, steel and particularly coal. The nearby Gower is an 18 mile long peninsula of limestone headlands and sandy bays; it is an area of

CAERNARFON CASTLE ▼

Y Gaer yn Arfon, meaning "Fort on the shore" in Welsh, sits on the tidal Menai Straits where the River Seiont runs into the sea. It was built by Edward I in two main stages between 1283 and 1323, but it was never finished despite its vast cost. The walls are up to 9ft thick and enclose an area of three acres—at one time they encircled the town of Caernarfon as well.

outstanding natural beauty. The once great industrial town of Merthyr Tydfil lies inland in the Taff Valley on the edge of a huge coalfield. In the mid-19th century iron made Merthyr the largest and most populous town in Wales and it became the largest steel and iron centre of manufacture in the world. But after World War I the heavy industry moved to the coast and the iron works closed in 1930. West Wales is altogether less developed although its wonderful coastline attracts visitors year-round. The small town of St. David's (after the patron saint of Wales), has a cathedral and was an important centre of Christianity in early

times. On the north Pembroke coast is Fishguard, from here boats cross the Irish Sea to Cork and Rosslare.

Mid-Wales is less discovered by visitors but there is plenty to see and do. Towns such as Llandrindod Wells and Builth Wells are ideal locations for exploring the wonderful surrounding countryside. To the south lie the Brecon Beacons National Park and east of them, the Black Mountains. North Wales, too. is mountainous with the massive presence of Snowdonia dominating all.

Caernarfon sits on the Menai Straits opposite the island of Anglesey. It is most famous for its huge fortified castle, built

by Edward I of England to establish his hold over the unruly Welsh.

Anglesey's main town is Holyhead. Early Christians settled here in the sixth century, and the church, although built much later, is still very old.

The centre of North Wales is Wrexham , not far from the border with England. Coal, iron and steel formed the backbone of Wrexham during Victorian times but these once huge industries have gone now and the town is much quieter for it. It has a magnificent ornamental church, the Church of St Giles, built in 1472 and considered one of the very finest in Wales.

SOUTH WALES

SEVERN ROAD BRIDGE ▲
The bridge linking England and Wales over the River Severn, or *Afon Hafren* in Welsh, took five years to build, between 1992 and 1996. The total length is just over 16,404ft, with a main span of 1,496ft in a main bridge of 3,107ft length. The number of approach spans is 45, divided between 22 at the Welsh end and 23 at the English.

NASH POINT ◀
The stratified cliffs of Nash Point are a designated heritage coast. The cliffs have been eroded by the waves to form a strange-looking series of steps.

CARDIFF HALL ▲

Situated in the heart of Cardiff,
St David's Hall is the National Concert
Hall and Conference Centre of Wales.

CARDIFF MILLENNIUM STADIUM ▶

Fifty-six thousand tonnes of concrete
and steel have created the new
Millennium Stadium which has risen
like a phoenix from the debris of the
old Arms Park rugby ground. The
retractable roof consists of two equal
panels 180ft by 249ft. The roof is parked
over the fixed roof of the north and
south stands. The roof panels meet at
the centre of the 364ft opening to form
a weatherproof covering.

WALES

THE MUMBLES ▲

The stone lighthouse on the outer island off Mumbles Head was first built in 1794. It had two platforms with a coal-fired beacon on each and was intended to warn shipping of the dangerous Mixon Sands and Cherry Stone rock. The Mumbles themselves are two small islands at the tip of Swansea Bay. The town of Oystermouth is in the foreground.

PENARTH MARINA ◄

Penarth Marina is situated within the sheltered waters of Cardiff Bay and built around the basins of the historic Penarth Docks.

NATIONAL BOTANIC GARDEN ▶

The National Botanic Garden of Wales, in Carmarthenshire is dedicated to science, education, and leisure alongside the broad study of plants and the environment.

MUSEUM OF WELSH LIFE ▼

The Museum of Welsh Life at St Fagan's, Cardiff, opened on July 7, 1948. Since then, it has established itself as one of Europe's foremost open-air museums, becoming Wales' most popular heritage attraction.

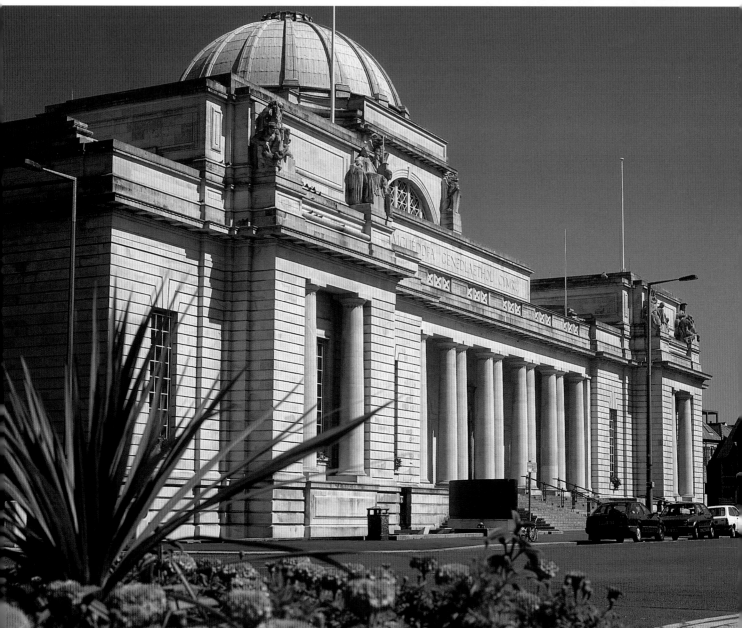

WALES

BRIDGEND ◀
An ancient town, Bridgend is also the administrative and holiday centre for the beautiful South Wales coastal area.

THREE CLIFFS BAY ▶
Three Cliffs Bay is one of the most photographed places on the Gower Peninsula. The cliffs themselves are very popular with climbers and are composed of three linked and pointed faces, their limestone strata punctured by a single tunneled archway that leads to the quiet Pobbles Beach.

WORMS HEAD ▲
The "Worm" is situated at the southern end of Rhosilli Bay and is only accessible two and a half hours either side of low water.

NEWPORT STEEL WAVE ▼
One of the most striking features of Newport is the extraordinary Steel Wave. Erected in 1990, Peter Fink's giant metal construction—built in recognition of Newport's debt to its steel industry—has become an integral feature of the Newport landscape.

WALES

DUFFRYN GARDENS ◀
These Grade I Listed Edwardian Gardens are in the process of being restored to the original design drawn up by Thomas Mawson in 1904.

LLANTHONY ▼
The great Celtic saint David was so taken by Llanthony that he built the first chapel there and called it Llanddewi Nant Hodi.

LLANDOVERY ▶

Two famous sons of Llandivery were notorious highwayman Twm Sion Cati (Thomas Jones, 1530–1609) and William Williams, Pantycelyn (1717–91) the Welsh hymn-writer who wrote the words translated as "Guide me o thou great redeemer".

LLYN Y FAN FACH ▼

The lake of Llyn y Fan Fach in the Carmarthenshire Black Mountain is the setting for one of the best known of all Welsh folktales. A local farmer falls in love with a woman who lives in the lake. She agrees to marry him but warns that she will leave him if he inflicts upon her "three causeless blows". They live happily for years and raise three sons. Three times, however, he strikes her accidentally with iron. She returns to the lake, taking her cattle with her.

WALES

BRYNGARW COUNTRY PARK ◀
Bryngarw's 113 acres are divided into
four areas—woodland, grassland, water
features, and formal gardens.

CAERPHILLY CASTLE ▼
Caerphilly was the first castle in Britain
to be built to a concentric design with
successive lines of defence set one inside
the other, so that when the attacker
stormed he would find himself face-to-
face with a second. Building started in
1268 by the Norman/English baron
Gilbert de Clare, Earl of Gloucester and
Hereford. Since the 15th century
Caerphilly has deteriorated and
Cromwell's troops even tried to dismantle it, luckily unsuccessfully. The
castle has been much restored in more
recent times.

LLANDAFF CATHEDRAL ▶

Llandaff Cathedral stands on one of the oldest Christian sites in Britain. In the sixth century St Dyfrig founded a community close to the ford where the Roman road crossed the River Taff. The present cathedral dates from c.1107-33 but it was not completed enough to dedicate until 1266.

LLANELLI PARC HOWARD ▼

Parc Howard houses a renowned collection of Llanelli Pottery (1839–1921), an art collection and material related to the history of the town.

WALES

MARGAM PARK ◀

This fantastic gothic mansion house boasts a magnificent orangery and is set in 850 acres of glorious parkland.

TAF FECHAN ▼

The Taf Fechan rises in the Brecon Beacons and is a major tributary to the River Taf. The nature reserve comprises about 1½ miles of winding river through steep carboniferous limestone gorges.

RHONDDA HERITAGE PARK ▶

The Rhondda Heritage Park is based at the former Lewis Merthyr Colliery, Trehafod.

RHOSSILI ▼

Famous for its spectacular beaches, Rhossili was also appreciated by prehistoric man. Two chambered tombs of rock were made on the landward slope of Rhossili Down by Stone Age men 6,000 years ago.

WALES

MERTHYR MAWR ◀
This small beauty spot is near Bridgend on the Ogmore river. In the grounds of the ruined oratory of St Roque's Chapel are some curious effigies and Celtic crosses. The nearby shore is remarkable for its extensive sand warrens, on the edge of which stand the remains of Candleston Castle, a fortified manor. Among the sand-hills have been discovered the remains of a large prehistoric burial-place.

WYE VALLEY FROM WYNDCLIFF ◀
Wye Valley and Vale of Usk is a land of magnificent scenery and the time-ravaged castles of the Welsh borderlands.

MONNOW BRIDGE ▼
Monnow Bridge and gate, Monmouth.

CRICKHOWELL ▶

Crickhowell is a market town situated between the Black Mountains and the Brecon Beacons.

BRECON CASTLE AND RIVER ▶

The castle was built by Bernard de Neufmarche, who took his name from the village of Neufmarche near Rouen, the capital of Normandy. He belonged to the second generation of conquerors who extended Norman influence into the Marches of Wales. By 1093 de Neufmarche and his knights had defeated the Welsh rulers of south Wales and began to build the castles from which they intended to control their new lands.

BEACONS NEAR LLANFRYNACH ▼

The Brecon Beacons National Park has sweeping mountains, lush green valleys and moorland full of history, geology, flora and fauna.

WEST WALES

ABERGLASNEY ◀

Spectacularly set in the beautiful Tywi valley of Carmarthenshire, Aberglasney Gardens have been an inspiration for poetry and gardeners since 1477.

ST. DAVID'S CATHEDRAL ▼

Built upon the site of St. David's sixth century monastery, St. Davids Cathedral has been a site of pilgrimage and worship for many hundreds of years and remains a church serving a living community.

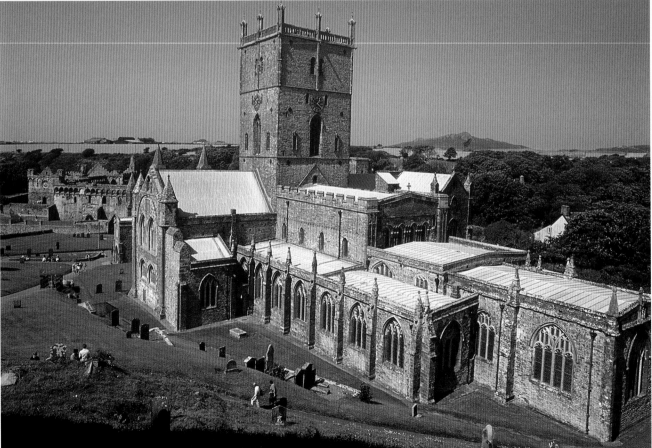

CARMARTHEN ▲

Carmarthenshire is a county with a beautiful coastline, castles, hills, villages where the Welsh language thrives, market towns with well-known national stores and attractive local shops, and plenty of outdoor activities. There are many tourist attractions well worth a visit such as the Millenium Coastal Path, the National Botanic Garden of Wales and Aberglasney Hall and Gardens.

CAREW CROSS ▶

The Cross is 14ft high and carved with intricate Celtic knots and ornaments and dates from the ninth century. It bears the Latin inscription *Margiteut Recett Rex*, celebrating an early Welsh king.

WALES

CAREW CASTLE ◀

Carew Castle is described by many as the "most handsome in all South Wales", and is also the site of the ancient Carew Cross.

FISHGUARD ▼

Fishguard and neighbouring Goodwick are said to have derived their names from the Vikings, who were frequent visitors to this part of the coast. The sheltered harbour at Lower Town was a bustling little cargo port with a fishing industry which made it famous from Elizabethan times for its herrings.

BURRY PORT ▶

Burry Port is a small picturesque town situated on the south-west coast of Wales.

STACK ROCKS ▼

Stack Rocks provides good views across to the Green Bridge of Wales, a magnificent natural limestone arch.

WALES

STRUMBLE HEAD ◀
The Pembrokeshire Coast Path runs all round this beautiful headland. The entire area is ideal for bird spotting—especially buzzards, peregrines, choughs, and a wide variety of sea birds.

TENBY HARBOUR ▼
The harbour has a unique backdrop of timeless buildings presented in an array of pastel colours.

WHITESANDS BAY ▶

One of the most popular beaches in all of Pembrokeshire, Whitesands is a large sandy beach surrounded by magnificent coastline, with views of Ramsey Island and several smaller islets out to sea. It is known for its sunsets all year round.

BARAFUNDLE ▼

East facing, so well sheltered from prevailing winds, Barafundle is owned and managed by the National Trust, and was originally part of the Stackpole estate, owned by the Cawdor family.

WALES

BOSHERSTON LAKES ◀
Created in the late 18th century by damming three narrow valleys, the lakes are now the centrepiece of an important National Nature Reserve.

DINEFWR PARK ▼
At the heart of Welsh history for a thousand years, Dinefwr Park took shape in the years after 1775, when the medieval castle, house, gardens, woods and deer park were integrated into one vast and breathtaking landscape

TEIFI VALLEY ▲

The River Teifi (TAY-VEE) is one of the longest rivers in Wales joining the Three counties on Pembrokeshire, Ceredigion and Carmarthenshire.

MANORBIER ▶

From its beginnings as a fortified manor house, Manorbier (roughly translated from ancient Welsh to mean "the estate of the Lords").

SKOMER ISLAND ▲

The island is a haven for wildlife and half a million seabirds breed here annually. Fulmars, guillemots, razorbills, kittiwakes, gulls, oystercatchers, curlew and short-eared owls are just some of the birdlife of the island. Dolphins, porpoises and grey seals are often seen crossing to and from the island in autumn and each year around 150 seal pups are born on the beaches and in the caves of Skomer.

PRESELI MOUNTAIN ▾

Legend was that bluestones from the Preseli Mountains were used in the construction of Stonehenge in Wiltshire—some 140 miles by sea and land. Amazingly, this fact was confirmed in modern times and it now seems certain that ancient Britons quarried the Preseli Mountains for their bluestones.

SAUNDERSFOOT ◀

Saundersfoot Bay Leisure Park is situated in a superb location in one of Wales' most beautiful settings, the Pembrokeshire Coastal National Park.

131

MID WALES

ABERDOVEY ◀

Aberdovey is a thriving little harbour resort set within the Snowdonia National Park, where the River Dovey meets the blue waters of Cardigan Bay.

MACHYNLLETH ▶

Machynlleth is the ancient capital of Wales, lying just south of the Snowdonia National Park.

DOLGELLAU ▶

Dolgellau is a small market town situated at the foot of the Cader Idris mountain range in south Snowdonia

ABERAERON ▶

A charming planned Georgian town located on Cardigan Bay. The well preserved Georgian facades are mainly painted with architectural details in a contrasting shade.

WALES

ABERYSTWYTH ◀

Aberystwyth is a small seaside town in the county of Ceredigion on the west coast of Wales. Situated towards the centre of the crescent of Cardigan Bay, Aberystwyth's harbour is fed by the confluence of the rivers Ystwyth and Rheidol.

BARMOUTH ▶

Barmouth's location on the west coast of North Wales and lying between a mountain range and the sea on the mouth of the River Mawddach is arguably one of the most beautiful locations in Wales. It rests just within the south-west corner of Snowdonia National Park and is steeped in a history rich with connections to the shipping and slate industries.

CWMTUDU ▼

The little hamlet of Cwmtudu has something of a smuggling past. The little cove and surrounding dark caves were ideal for ships to arrive at the dead of night with their cargoes of salt and brandy. Ships would also arrive with limestone from South Wales which was brought ashore to be burnt in the old lime-kiln that is set back from the beach.

DEVILS BRIDGE FALLS ▶

Devil's Bridge is situated high in the foothills of the Pumlumon mountain range twelve miles east of Aberystwyth

HARLECH ▼

Spectacularly sited, Harlech Castle seems to grow naturally from the rock on which it is perched. Like an all-seeing sentinel, it gazes out across land and sea, keeping a watchful eye over Snowdonia.

YNYS LOCHTYN ◀
At Llangrannog a spectacular walk along the cliffs leads to the National Trust promontory at Ynys Lochtyn.

MWNT ▼
The beautiful beach of Mwnt has the finest views over Cardigan Bay.

NEW QUAY ▲

Ceinewydd in Welsh, New Quay climbs a hill overlooking Cardigan Bay Bottlenose dolphins can be observed from the shore.

CABAN COCH ELAN VALLEY ▶

The lowest of the dams in the sequence of four built in the valley of the Elan River is Caban Coch dam. The lake formed is nearly 500 acres in size.

WALES

CRAIG GOCH ▲

The dam at Craig Goch, the highest upstream of the series of dams in the Elan Valley, is often referred to as the top dam. It is located at a height of 1,040 feet (317m) above sea level.

LAKE VYRNWY ◀

Lake Vyrnwy is man-made, with the dam that created it completed in 1888. The village of Llanwddyn was submerged by the lake, which is one of the biggest man-made likes in Wales.

LLYN BRIANNE ◥

Llyn Brianne is situated on the headwaters of the River Towy, near its source in the Cambrian Mountains. Beautiful, romantic and still quite unspoilt the Towy rises some way up the valley past Nantystalwyn,

LLYNNAU CREGENNEN ▶

The Llynnau Cregennen are two tarns high up—some 800ft behind Arthog—on the western slopes of the Cadair Idris range, overlooking the Mawddach estuary.

MAWDDACH RIVER ▲

This nature reserve is situated in the superb scenery of the Mawddach Valley and offers beautiful walks through oak woodland. In the spring pied flycatchers, wood warblers and redstarts can be seen and heard in the wood.

AFON BANWY ◀

Rural in character, this thinly populated central region is the most peaceful and least explored part of Wales.

BERRIEW

Berriew means the place where the
Rhiw flows into the River Secern. At
the confluence is a village in the heart
of the Welsh border country, a few miles
southwest of Welshpool. A fertile area,
Berriew was prosperous in the 18th and
19th centuries and many cottages from
this period survive.

DYLIFE ▼

Nestled away in the mountains of mid-
Wales is the quiet town of Dylife—
"Place of Floods"—on the Plynlimon
escarpment.

WALES

STRATA FLORIDA ▲

Ruins of the abbey at Strata Florida. The unusual name is a Latinized from of the Welsh *Ystrad Fflur* (meaning wide valley or plain of flowers). The Abbey was founded by the Cistercian Order in ll64 though there is evidence of an earlier Cluniac settlement nearby. Strata Florida was dissolved by Henry VIII in 1539.

LLANDDEWI BREFI ◀

A pretty rural village, Llanddewi Brefi is noted for its handsome church on the site of which St David is reputed to have performed a miracle.

LLANDRINDOD WELLS ▶

Llandrindod Wells has been the county town of Powys since 1974 and prior to that was the administrative centre for the County of Radnor.

LLANGRANNOG ▶

Llangrannog has a special significance within Wales for nearby is a residential facility operated by Urdd Gobaith Cymru—Wales's League of Youth. Generation after generation of Welsh children have spent a holiday here and the wonderful range of sports and leisure facilities on offer by the Urdd (pronounced "Eerthe")—including a dry ski slope.

LLANIDLOES ▶

Wales' only remaining Market Hall (built in 1609) which houses an internationally renowned Quilts Exhibition, stands at the centre of the town. Llanidloes most significant moment came in 1839 when, as an important weaving centre, it became a hotbed of Chartists. The ensuing fracas led to a number of men being sent to Australia for 15 years.

NORTH WALES

One of Wales' best beaches and most romantic locations.

Portmeirion ▼

An Italianate village, famous as the setting for the cult television series "The Prisoner", that starred Patrick McGoohan, Portmeirion was designed by Clough Williams-Ellis. It has other film involvement—Noel Coward's *Blythe Spirit* was written there.

AMLWCH ▶

Amlwch is situated on the north-eastern corner of Anglesey. A small town with a long history of working traditions dating back to the Bronze Age when it was an important location for trading the copper from Anglesey's Parys Mountain mines..

BEAUMARIS ▲

King Edward I built a magnificent castle at Beaumaris on the Menai Straits. The town is interesting, too: explore the atmospheric interiors of the Victorian Gaol and Courthouse.

MENAI BRIDGE ▼

The total length of the bridge is 1,500ft; part of which is supported by the three arched piers on the mainland side and four piers on the Anglesey side. The suspended span between the two "pyramids", one of which rests on Ynys Y Moch, is 580ft.

WALES

LLANFAIR PG

Its full name is "Llanfairpwllgwyngyll gogerychwyrndrobwllllantysilio- gogogoch". It was reputedly invented by an Innkeeper during the last century to drum up more trade from train travellers.

LLANDUDNO ▶

Llandudno is Wales's largest resort, uniquely situated between the Great and Little Ormes with two wonderful beaches, the award-winning North Shore and the quiet, sand-duned West Shore.

LLANDDWYN ISLAND ◀

Llanddwyn is not quite an island: it remains attached to the mainland at all but the highest tides. It provides excellent views of Snowdonia and the Lleyn Peninsula and is part of the Newborough Warren National Nature Reserve.

ABERDARON ▶

Aberdaron is an old whitewashed fishing village. Situated at the western tip of North Wales, its church is extraordinarily old, dating back to the Celtic era before the mission of St Augustine in the late seventh century.

WHISTLING SANDS ▲
At Porth Oer, 2.5 miles north-west of
Aberdaron, are Whistling Sands, so
called because they seem to whistle
when walked upon.

SOUTH STACK ◀
Over 4,000 pairs of seabirds breed on
the cliffs at South Stack every year.
Between April and July you can watch
them from the Ellin's Tower centre.
During the breeding season you can see
puffins, fulmars, guillemots and razorbills.

PENRHYN CASTLE ▶

Penrhyn Castle is situated between Snowdonia and the Menai Strait, and it is a fine piece of neo-Norman architecture, built between 1827 and 1846.

BETWS-Y-COED ▼

Betws-y-Coed is the principal village of the Snowdonia National Park. It is the perfect centre to use to explore the jewel of North Wales: Snowdon itself.

WALES

Bodnant Garden ▲

One of the world's most spectacular gardens, situated above the River Conwy with stunning views across Snowdonia, Bodnant was laid out in 1847 and given to the National Trust in 1949 by Lord Aberconway.

Conwy ◀

Conwy is the classic walled town. Its circuit of walls, over three-quarters of a mile long and guarded by no fewer than 22 towers, is one of the finest in the world.

CONWY VALLEY ▶

The valley proper begins at the Conwy Falls situated above the confluence with the River Lledr close to Betws-y-Coed, the starting point for many forest and lake walks.

LLANRWST ▼

Llanrwst is situated in the Conwy Valley to the north of Betws-y-Coed.

WALES

CONWY CASTLE ▲
Conwy is by any standards one of the great fortresses of medieval Europe. Built by Edward I to protect his interests against the last of the independent Welsh princes, Llywelyn, Conwy today is also kown for Telford's suspension bridge built across the estuary in 1827.

ABERGLASLYN PASS ◄
Aberglaslyn Pass is known for its impressive waterfalls, Sygun Copper Mine and the spectacular scenery of the unspoilt Lleyn Peninsula.

ABERSOCH ▶

Abersoch is situated on the Llyn Peninsula in North Wales and has become a very popular village seaside resort.

LLANBERIS LAKE RAILWAY ▼

Starting at Gilfach Ddu station ("Gilvak Thee") in the Padarn Park at Llanberis, the trains take approximately 40 minutes to make the journey to Penllyn and back, including a short stop at Cei Llydan ("Kai Thlidan") for sightseeing on the homeward run.

WALES

Llanbedrog ◀

Llanbedrog is one of the key centers of the unique Lleyn Peninsula, a dem-paradise tucked away beyond the mighty mountains of Snowdonia. It is especially renowned for its sheltered sandy beaches nestling under a steep rocky headlands covered with pictur-esque heather and fringed by pine trees.

Porth Dinllaen ◀

On the north-facing coast of the Lleyn Peninsula, the remote 18th-century fishing village of Porth Dinllaen nestles on the edge of a beautiful beach.

Pwllheli ◤

Hafan Pwllheli is situated on the south side of the Lleyn and is the capital of the peninsula. It provides access to some of the best sailing waters in the UK including Cardigan Bay, Anglesey and the attractive harbours along Ireland's east coast.

Beddgelert ▶

Gelert's Grave is named after the faith-ful hound of Prince Llywelyn the Great. Llywelyn returned home to find his hound Gelert, whom he had left to protect his son, covered with gore. Fearing the worst he slew his hound only to discover later that the blood was from the wolf faithful Gerlert had killed in defence of Llywelyn's heir..

CAERNARFON ▲

Lying on the Menai Straits where the River Seiont reaches the sea, Caernarfon was settled by the Celts before the Romans came or before Edward I built his great castle there.

CEIRIOG VALLEY ◄

The Ceiriog Valley is a place of mountains and valleys, rivers and waterfalls. It is bounded by the rugged grandeur of the Berwyn Mountains, rising at Cader Fronwen to some 2,300ft and by the tributaries of the Vyrnwy and Severn rivers.

LLYN GWYNANT ▶

Lake Gwynant is one of Snowdonia's lakes with a fantastic view of the main mountain.

VALLE CRUCIS ABBEY ▼

Near Llangollen, Valle Crucis was founded in 1189 and dissolved by Henry VIII. What's left shows off the Early English style of architecture..

LLECHWEDD SLATE CAVERNS ◀

Llechwedd Slate Caverns offer a choice of two spectacular rides into the vast slate mines of Blaenau Ffestiniog.

MOEL FAMMAUE ◀

Wales is green and lush in the summer and this photograph shows the typical scenery of the old Kingdom of Gwynedd which covered north-west Wales.

PARYS MOUNTAIN ▲

A hill rich in copper and very profitably mined from earliest times, Parys Mountain was particularly important during the Industrial Revolution.

PISTYLL RHAEADR ▶

Best visited from Llanfyllin, Pistyll Rhaeadr is the "Hidden Pearl of Wales".

RUTHIN ◀

The town of Ruthin was built on a red sandstone hill as a strategic lookout over the River Clwyd. A town which has over 700 years of recorded history, whose streets have been trodden by kings, queens, princes and travellers; its past suffered plague, battle and siege; its buildings reflect the best of architectural styles making the town an outstanding Conservation Area worthy of preservation.

SWALLOW FALLS ▶

The Swallow Falls is probably Wales' most famous waterfall.

YR EIFL ▼

Yr Eifl above Llanaelhaern boasts one of Britain's most spectacular hillforts— Tre'r Ceiri.

SCOTLAND

SCOTLAND

SHOOTING HUT NEAR LAKE ◀
One of the great Scottish passions is fishing, whether it be in the rivers and streams, lochs, sea fishing or in a quiet backwater where only the sounds of nature break the silence.

SCOTTISH BARONIAL ▶
Scottish architects developed a distinctive style of fortified and turretted castle for their wealthy clients.

Scotland is an ancient kingdom stretching far north of England and out across the hostile seas to numerous islands beyond the mainland. The land is full of history and legend as well as mountain ranges and deep lochs. Much of the country is uninhabited by anything except a few farmers and wildlife. In the Highlands and islands life has always been hard, scraping a living from the unforgiving land has made the Scots a tough race

Each area has its own special character; for example, Dumfries and Galloway lie in the south of Scotland, just next to the border with England. With over 200 miles of dramatic coastline, majestic wild mountains, and heather clad moorlands, this is an unspoilt countryside and natural environment. This is Robert Burns territory where you can visit his house, his mausoleum, and his favourite pub. To the south sits medieval Caerlaverock Castle and the nearby nature reserve, also the village of Kirkbean, birthplace of John Paul Jones, founding father of the American Navy. His adventurous life is

recounted in a museum which includes a recreation of his cabin on board his flagship the *Bonhomme Richard*.

Just across the border from England lies the Land of the Border Reivers. The lands were lawless and bitter family feuds over land ownership on both sides of the border terrorised the country folk. In the 15th and 16th centuries life here was marked by cattle rustling, blackmail, murder and mayhem. In feuding times, farming families built fortified tower houses for protection. In the towns, mounted militia stood at the ready to repel invaders.

In Lothian lies Edinburgh, the capital of Scotland, and this magnificent city never fails to captivate the visitor. Edinburgh's festival spirit extends far beyond the famous International and Fringe Festivals held every summer. The area is full of fantastic castles, great houses, and miles of glorious coastline. It's also the ancient home of the game of golf. Some of the great links and parkland courses of the world are here—such as the championship courses at Muirfield

and Dalmaho. Golf was first recorded in Musselburgh, just outside Edinburgh, and on Leith Links the gentlemen of the Edinburgh Club first drew up the rules of the game. Links after links follow the sandy coastline east from the city, while in the rolling countryside to the south and west there are fine parkland courses

Glasgow is Scotland's largest city and is one of the liveliest and most cosmopolitan destinations in Europe—a city of culture and design. It is an impressive city architecturally and was home to one of the greatest British architects and designers —Charles Rennie Macintosh.

The Highland Boundary Fault separates Highland and Lowland Scotland and passes right through Perthshire. When the Romans reached Britain, they marched as far north as Perthshire, but could not conquer the fiercely proud people they encountered. It is rumoured that, at one of their patrol outposts, near the village of Fortingall, one Pontius Pilate was born, son of a Roman general stationed there at the time. Some of the earliest inhabitants of Scotland, the Picts

SOUTH OF SCOTLAND

also left their mark—literally. Carved and sculptured stones are dotted around as testimony to this mysterious race and kingdom about all too little is known.

The Aberdeen and Grampian region is blessed with outstanding scenery and a tranquil environment. So much so that it has attracted visitors for more than 150 years. Indeed, Queen Victoria wrote in her private journal, "It seems like a dream to be here in our dear Highland home again. Every year my heart becomes more fixed in this dear Highland paradise."

The Scottish Highlands have a special magic all their own. Spectacular mountains, tumbling rivers, and mirror-like lochs are bounded by crystal-clear seas scattered with mysterious islands. A remarkable variety of wildlife makes its home in the glens and sea-lochs where an unbroken thread of human history reaches back into the mists of time.

Scotland is fringed with numerous islands and the Clan Donald chose well when they made Islay the centre of their vast Lordship of the Isles. Rich pasturelands play host each autumn to clouds of

geese arriving for the winter while locally cut peat gives a unique flavour to the Islay malts. Nearby Jura is sparsely populated with its "Paps", or mountains, the province of eagles and deer.

Across the sea on the Isle of Skye and in the land of Lochalsh there are plenty of historic castles and standing stones, craft shops, and old croft museums, and above all amazing scenery. This island has a rich, if sometimes cruel, history and is an island of rough textures, soft colours and fine light, an island of strong traditions and a thriving Gaelic culture.

The seventy or so islands that comprise Orkney are known as the Outer Isles and are best known for Neolithic remains. Orkney's history has been nothing less than dramatic—providing endless raw material for the islands' natural born storytellers.

South Ronaldsay is the nearest Orkney Island to mainland Scotland, just across the Pentland Firth from John O'Groats. The main town is St. Margarets Hope. The islands of Burray and South Ronaldsay are paradise for birdwatchers.

Hoy means "High Island" from the Old Norse *haey*. It is the second largest island in Orkney at 57 square miles. The north and west are hilly and more "Highland" in character, the south and east low-lying and fertile, more typical of Orkney in general.

Over a hundred islands make up Shetland. The first Norsemen who came here were farmers as well as Vikings. They settled on fertile ground overlooking bays and brought with them a new style of building, a political system, laws, and a new language. Missionaries later arrived and Christianity spread rapidly.

Shetland became part of Scotland in the late 14th century as part of the dowry of Margaret, daughter of the king of Denmark, on her marriage to king James III of Scotland. Since then, Scottish influence has prevailed over the islands.

In short, wherever you travel in Scotland, you are surrounded by a landscape that is drenched in history and incident, where everywhere you look and everything you see has a tale to tell and a song to sing.

SCOTLAND

VILLAGE BY WATER ▲

The lochs and coastline of Scotland have played a significant role in the local economy through the fishing industry.

BROUGHTON HOUSE ◀

The 18th-century town house of the Murrays of Broughton and Cally was bought in 1901 by E. A. Hornel, the renowned artist and member of "The Glasgow Boys". Between 1901 and 1933 he added an art gallery and studio overlooking the fascinating Japanese influenced garden, which leads down to the Dee estuary. The house contains many of Hornel's works as well as paintings by other artists, and an extensive collection of Scottish books.

CAERLAVEROCK CASTLE ◀

Caerlaverock was besieged by Edward I in 1300 and held by the English until 1312 when the keeper switched allegiance to the Robert the Bruce. The English laid siege again to reclaim the castle, but failed to take it. Later the keeper, Sir Eustace Maxwell, was ordered by Robert the Bruce to dismantle it to prevent any future use by the English.

DRAFT MENNOCK PASS ▲

The Mennock Pass begins its descent from Wanlockhead and follows the flow of the Mennock Burn, where visitors can often be seen panning for gold. The heather-clad hills on either side contain a palpable air of mystery. Tales of past times abound—the Covenanters' Pulpit and Watchman's Knowe near the top of Beir Burn are silent testament to the Covenanters who worshipped and farmed around here.

RUTHWELL ▶

The Ruthwell Cross stands in a small church in the town of Ruthwell, just south of Dumfries, in south-west Scotland. The Cross is 17ft 4in tall and sits in a well 4ft deep to serve as the high cross for the church. With the comparable cross at Bewcastle it is undoubtedly the most important sculptural survival from the distant times of Anglo-Saxon Britain.

KIPPFORD ▶

Also known as Scaur, the village of Kippford in Dumfries and Galloway lies at the mouth of the Urr Water, 5 miles (8 km) south of Dalbeattie. At Kippford is a tidal estuary running into the Solway and inland sailing on Loch Ken.

SAMYE LING MONKS, ESKDALEMUIR ▲

Samye Ling in Dumfries is a world centre for Tibetan Buddhism. The community (much of which is still under construction) consists of an extraordinary and inspiring temple. On the hill and out of bounds lies the area where devotees retreat to contemplate in complete peace and serenity surrounded by inspiring countryside.

DRUMLANRIG CASTLE ▲

Belonging to the Duke of Buccleuch and Queensberry this magnificent 1680s castle is built of pink sandstone on the duke's ancestral Douglas lands. Inside the castle are splendid rooms containing many historic treasures, including paintings, silver, porcelain, and fine furniture. As well as the castle there are plenty of other attractions including the gardens, a cycle museum, craft workshops, tearoom, adventure playground, and woodland and riverside walks.

ST. NINIANS CAVE ◀

St. Ninian's Cave lies near Whithorn, Scotland's oldest town and the cradle of Christianity in Scotland. The cave is said to have been used by St. Ninian as a retreat and is still a holy site and place of pilgrimage.

DOCK PARK ◀

Dock Park in the fall. trampolines, putting green, two bowling greens, crazy golf, swing ball and tennis courts

BURNS' COTTAGE ▲

Situated 22 miles to the north of Girvan lies the modest home of the great Scottish poet Robert Burns.

TUNBERRY HOTEL ▼

Home of one of the most famous golf courses in the world Turnberry has hosted many amateur and professional golf championships, culminating in its first Open Championship in 1977.

ORCHARDTON TOWER ▲

Situated outside Palnackie in Dumfries and Galloway, Orchardton Tower is the only example of a round tower-house in Scotland. It is believed to have been built in the 1450s for John Cairns, although it passed into Maxwell family hands in 1633. Its most famous resident was Sir Robert Maxwell who featured in Sir Walter Scott's novel *Guy Mannering*. Ownership has now passed to Historic Scotland.

CULZEAN CASTLE ▲

Built 1772–1790 by Robert Adam for David, 10th Earl of Cassillis on a cliff-top site associated with the Kennedy family since the late 14th century. It contains an Eisenhower Room recalling the president's links with Scotland.

MACHRIE MOOR STANDING STONES, ISLE OF ARRAN ◀

The whole moorland is littered with the remains of early man, from hut circles to chambered cairns and solitary standing stones. The focus of the site is concentrated in a small area of the moorland and consists of six stone circles of varying structure.

HOME OF JOHN DAVIDSON ▼

The village souter (shoemaker), and the original "Souter Johnnie" of Robert Burns' *Tam o' Shanter*. The refurbished thatched cottage contains Burns relics, period furniture, and a reconstructed souter's workshop.

ST. ABBS HEAD ▶

St. Abbs Head is dramatically situated between farmland and the North Sea. Higher up the cliffs are the homes of colonies of guillemots, kittiwakes, shags, razorbills, fulmars, puffins, and herring gulls, which nest on narrow ledges from April to August. St Abb's Head was declared a National Nature Reserve in 1983 and is the most important location of cliff-nesting seabirds in southeast Scotland.

DUNDONALD CASTLE ◀

The hill on which Dundonald stands has a been occupied since c.2000BC. Nothing survives of the first castle built around the mid-12th century, probably by Walter Stewart, first Steward of Scotland. It was replaced in the late 13th century by a much larger stone castle consisting of two large blocks facing each other across a circular courtyard and four round towers at intervals in a high curtain wall.

KELSO ▶

This ••• town has a rich historic tradition as evidenced by the Romanesque Kelso Abbey (?) built in 1128 and the memorial cloister to the 8th Duke of Roxburgh. Floors Castle— the largest inhabited house in Scotland —can clearly be seen from Kelso Bridge and further afield is the site of the town of Roxburgh with its castle, first recorded as the residence of the Earl of Northumberland in 1107.

RIVER TWEED ▲

Flowing east from its source in the
Southern Uplands, the Tweed is about
97 miles long and is one of the major
salmon rivers of Scotland with ninety
plus miles of rod fishing. The lower part
is generally classed as the border
between Scotland and England, though
the true border is slightly further north.

DRUMLANRIGS TOWER, HAWICK ▶

A stronghold of cross-border warfare, it
was converted into a gracious hotel in
the 1930's.

WILTON LODGE PARK ◀

The park sits beside the River Teviot's
wooded banks and extends to over 107
acres, with riverside and tree lined
walks, picnic tables, recreational facilities
and a walled garden. In the park a
statue commemorates the life of Jimmie
Guthrie, ace TT rider and world
champion during the 1930's. Nearby
the imposing Hawick museum and
Scott Gallery document the town's
diverse history.

JEDBURGH ABBEY ▲
Founded by David I in 1138 for Augustinian canons, on the edge of the frontier with England. The church is mostly Romanesque and early Gothic in style and is remarkably complete, given the rough treatment it received over the centuries by a succession of English invasion forces.

KIRKHOPE TOWER ▶

MANDERSTON ▼
A house on which no expense was spared with opulent staterooms, the only silver-staircase in the world and extensive 'downstairs' domestic quarters. It stands in 56 acres of formal gardens, with magnificent stables and stunning marble dairy.

MELLERSTAIN ▲
Unique because for nearly fifty years it was two houses. Designed by William Adam in 1725, two wings were built by Lord Haddington's ancestor, George Baillie. Adam also designed a central block, but this was never built.

JEDBURGH ◄
The young Mary Queen of Scots' arrived in Jedburgh in 1566 to hold a Circuit Court, and a 16th century bastel house (fortified house) was put at her disposal. Hearing that her lover Bothwell lay wounded at Hermitage Castle in Liddesdale, Mary set out on an arduous return journey of 40 miles to visit him. She came back from the moorland ride, ill and close to death and is later said to have remarked "Would that I had died at Jedburgh," as troubles crowded upon her.

MAILROS ABBEY AND ST CUTHBERT'S CHAPEL ◄
Old Melrose lies on the peninsula formed by a wide eastwards bend of the River Tweed cutting into Bemersyde Hill. On the hill is the famous Scott's View overlooking the Tweed and the Mailros site.

PAXTON HOUSE ▶

Built by the Adam brothers in 1758 for
the young Patrick Home it is one of the
finest examples anywhere of an 18th
century Palladian country house.

PEEBLES ▼

The local motto "Peebles for Pleasure" is
borne out by the town's attractive setting
among the hills on the banks of the
River Tweed.

ST. MARY'S LOCH ▼ ▼

St. Mary's Loch is set in the heart of the
Southern Scottish Uplands in the
Scottish Borders.

PRINCES STREET ◀

Edinburgh's main thoroughfare has been described as one of the most beautiful streets in the world. Its fame springs, of course, not from its imposing architecture but from the street's incomparable setting. Princes Street is as fine a boulevard as will be encountered anywhere.

Old Town from Princes Street ▶

The Old and New Towns of Edinburgh are a designated World Heritage Site. The great castle dominates Edinburgh and the city itself boasts magnificent architecture from the lofty buildings of its medieval Old Town, as they tumble down the spine of the Royal Mile, to the grace of the Georgian New Town. Every step is a revelation—an alleyway that reveals an ancient courtyard, or a wynd that opens up a new panorama. The Old Town is the heart of Scotland's capital city. It plays a key role in respect to civic, legal, religious, and cultural activities both nationally and in the life of the City of Edinburgh.

EDINBURGH AND LOTHIANS

CHARLOTTE SQUARE ◀ ◀

Robert Adam's last commission. These elegant town houses attracted wealthy people from the Old Town tenements.

VICTORIA STREET ◀

The Grassmarket area has had a market dating back several hundred years.

FORTH ROAD BRIDGE ▶

This landmark has dominated the local view since it was opened in 1890 by the Prince of Wales.

ROYAL MILE ◀

A number of connected streets, starting at Edinburgh Castle that runs downhill from west to east, starting with Castle Hill, followed by the Camera Obscura.

THE GEORGIAN HOUSE ◀

The Georgian House is part of 26-31 Charlotte Square and dates from 1796. The house's beautiful china, shining silver, exquisite paintings, and furniture all reflect the domestic surroundings and social conditions for wealthy Scots of that time.

THE HUB AND CAMERA OBSCURA ▶

These two early 17th-century tenements were added to by an optician in the middle of the 19th century to become Short's Observatory, whose crowning glory was the Camera Obscura.

EDINBURGH CASTLE ▼

Perched on top of an extinct volcanic plug 443ft above sea level and 33ft above the street, it is easy to appreciate why this site was chosen some 3,000 years ago as the place to build a stronghold.

SCOTLAND

CALTON HILL ◄

Calton Hill is one of Edinburgh's main hills, set right in the city centre. It is unmistakable with its Athenian acropolis poking above the skyline.

HOLYROOD PALACE ◄

At the end of the Royal Mile, situated in the shadow of Arthur's Seat, the Palace of Holyroodhouse is closely associated with Scotland's turbulent past. Mary Queen of Scots lived here between 1561 and 1567. She married two of her husbands in the Abbey and witnessed the murder of her private secretary, David Rizzio, in her Outer Chamber.

TANTALLON CASTLE ◄

The coastal fortress of Tantallon Castle was built around 1350 by William 1st Earl of Douglas, nephew of "Good Sir James." The design of the castle was originally based on a French chateau.

Borthwick Castle ▲

Borthwick Castle is a magnificent stone enclosure fortress, one of the most impressive in Scotland. The massive U-plan keep stands inside a walled courtyard, with round towers at the corners, only one of which remains.

North Berwick Harbor ▶

The famous engineer Robert Stevenson (whose work included the Bell Rock lighthouse and the eastward extension of Princes Street in Edinburgh towards Calton Hill) spent many summers at Anchor Villa in North Berwick. During the 1860s he shared the holiday home with three generations of his remarkable family, including his young grandson Robert Louis Stevenson.

Bass Rock, North Berwick ▲

The Bass Rock is the closest sea bird sanctuary to the mainland and was the first to be studied by ornithologists during the 19th century, when they gave the Gannet the scientific name *Sula bassana*. The colony holds approximately 10 percent of the world population of North Atlantic Gannets.

Salisbury Crags ▶

Salisbury Crag is located on the West side of Holyrood Park

SCOTLAND

RIVER CLYDE ▲

Glasgow's early importance and wealth was due to its location on the western side of Britain which enabled easy and lucrative trade with the New World. Wealth came to the city via the River Clyde in the 18th century, thanks to the tobacco and cotton trade with Virginia. Other important imports were sugar and rum from the West Indies. In Victorian times Glasgow developed a huge heavy industry thanks to vast local deposits of coal and iron ore. This brought ship building, engineering—especially the building of railroad locomotives—and the steel industry.

THE SECC, GLASGOW ◀

The SECC is the largest integrated exhibition and conference centre and Scotland's national venue for public events.

GLASGOW AND CLYDE VALLEY

GLASGOW CATHEDRAL ▶

The first stone built cathedral was dedicated in 1136 in the presence of King David I but this has been a Christian site for well over 1,500 years. The cathedral is dedicated to St. Mungo and was built between the 12th and 15th centuries, although most of the fittings inside are now 19th century,

GALLERY OF MODERN ART ▶

Exhibits include works by Niki de Saint Phalle, David Hockney, Sebastiao Salgado, Andy Warhol, and Eduard Bersudsky as well as Scottish artists such as John Bellany and Ken Curry.

UNIVERSITY OF GLASGOW ▲
The university dates from 1451 when the Scottish king James II persuaded Pope Nicholas V to grant a bull authorising Bishop Turnbull of Glasgow to set up a university. Glasgow remains a university in the great European tradition.

GLASGOW SCIENCE CENTRE ▼
Glasgow Science Centre is Scotland's flagship Millennium Project. Housed in three stunning buildings at Pacific Quay on the Clyde, GSC brings science and technology to life through hundreds of interactive exhibits in the Science Mall and the unique experiences of the GSC IMAX® Theatre and the Glasgow Tower.

TALL SHIP ▲
The Tall Ship offers the chance to explore one of the last remaining Clyde built tall ships, the s.v. *Glenlee* (1896).

NEW LANARK WORLD HERITAGE VILLAGE ▲

The historic village of New Lanark, founded as a brand new industrial settlement in 1785 is still a living, working community, and has recently been awarded World Heritage Status. It became world-famous as a model community under the enlightened regime of the social and educational pioneer Robert Owen, who owned and managed the water-powered cotton mills from 1800-1825.

POLLOK HOUSE ◄

The Maxwell family have lived here since the mid-13th century. Three earlier castles were replaced by the present house (c.1740) after consultation with William Adam. The house was extended in 1890 by Sir John Stirling Maxwell, and now contains an internationally famed collection of paintings as well as porcelain and furnishings appropriate to a country house of the Edwardian period. It is set within Pollok Country Park, also home of The Burrell Collection.

THE MACKINTOSH HOUSE ▶

The Mackintosh House is a faithful reconstruction of the principal interiors from the Glasgow home of the great Scottish architect and designer Charles Rennie Mackintosh (1868-1928) and his wife the acclaimed artist Margaret Macdonald Mackintosh (1864-1933).

SCOTLAND

GREENBANK GARDEN ◄
Greenbank garden contains 2½ acres of
walled garden and 15 acres of surrounding grounds. The elegant Georgian
house was built in 1764 for a wealthy
Glasgow merchant.

ART GALLERY & MUSEUM ▼
The world famous Glasgow Art Gallery
and Museum are housed in an imposing
red sandstoned building that was first
opened in 1901. Today it shows a
superb collection of paintings by, among
others, Botticelli, Rembrandt, Monet,
van Gogh, and Picasso.

TINTO HILL ▶
Tinto Hill rises to 2,320ft and is close to Symington in Upper Clydesdale. It gets its name from the red feldspar rock.

CLOCH LIGHTHOUSE & CLYDE ESTUARY ▼
One of the most distinctive landmarks on the Clyde estuary is the Cloch Lighthouse at Cloch Point, directly opposite Dunoon. Returning sailors and voyagers knew that they were nearly home when they rounded the Cloch and entered the Clyde.

SCOTLAND

THE HEBRIDEAN ISLANDS ◀

Islay and Jura lie off the coast of Argyll, on the west coast of Scotland. They can be reached easily by air from Glasgow, or by car ferry from the Kintyre peninsula. On a clear day the coast of Ireland can be seen in the distance.

CALLENDAR HOUSE ▼

Built in the style of a French chateau and set in the magnificent grounds of Falkirk's Callendar Park, Callendar House has long played a major role in the area and Scotland's history, through wars, rebellions, and the Industrial Revolution, and has played host to many great historical figures over the centuries, such as Mary Queen of Scots, Cromwell, and Bonnie Prince Charlie.

ARGYLL

STIRLING CASTLE ▶
Imposingly situated at the head of
Stirling's Old Town, the castle is
mounted high on an old volcanic
outcrop. The first references to Stirling
Castle appear in early 12th century.

INVERARAY CASTLE, INVERARAY ▼
A fine early example of Scottish
Baronial style built in the mid 18th
century on the site of an earlier building.

SCOTLAND

JURA FROM ISLAY, HEBRIDES ◀
Lying off the coast of Argyll, on the west coast of Scotland, they can be reached easily by air from Glasgow, or by car ferry from the Kintyre peninsula. On a clear day the coast of Ireland can be seen in the distance.

BALQUHIDDER GLEN ▼
Although its origins are lost in the mists of time, Balquhidder has in all liklihood been important since Neolithic times. Below the Manse there are remains of a stone circle, the Pudreag Stone, and there is a Neolithic chambered cairn nearby.

KILCHURN CASTLE ▲

This splendid ruin sits on a small peninsula along the marshy banks of Loch Awe. Originally built as a five storey Tower House (still surviving) the castle was remodelled many times throughout its 250 year history.

LOCH LOMOND ◀

Loch Lomond is the largest fresh water loch in Great Britain. The Loch is some 24 miles long and five miles wide and at its deepest point is some 600 feet deep.

ARDUAINE GARDEN ▼

This 20 acre garden on the Sound of Jura lies on the south slope of a promontory between Loch Melfort and Asknish Bay and benefits from the warmth of the Gulf Stream.

Ben Cruachan ▲

Ben Cruachan is a mountain of stunning peaks and ridges combined with views out to sea and up Loch Etive. It rises to a sharp peak at 3,694ft. The main spine of the mountain runs east to west above Loch Awe. High up the slopes an open corrie has been dammed to form the Cruachan Reservoir.

Wallace Monument ◀

William Wallace was born around 1274 and was drawn into the campaign for Scottish independence from the English after the death of king Alexander III in 1286. Wallace's most successful battle was at Stirling Bridge in 1296. However, he was betrayed and executed in London in 1305. His monument is on the hill of Abbey Craig. There are 246 steps up the spiral staircase to the top of the monument from which magnificent views over the River Forth can be enjoyed.

GLENCOE ▲

The hills of Glencoe are significant as
an example of a volcano collapsing in
on itself during a series of violent
eruptions many millennia ago. This is
also an area of international botanical
importance, particularly for the
woodlands and arctic alpine flora, but it
is for the awful Glencoe Massacre in
17★★ that the area is infamous.

LOCH AWE ▶

Some 24 miles long and quite narrow,
Loch Awe forms a considerable
catchment area for the many feeder
burns flowing from the surrounding
mountains such as Ben Cruachan. The
water quality is particularly high and
the fish population thrive in this rich,
natural feeding area.

SCOTLAND

RUMBLING BRIDGE ▼

Another highlight area to explore on foot is Rumbling Bridge. Lovely views and stunning scenery are the order of the day here as in so many areas in Scotland. White water canoeing is popular in many of the rivers around here but this one is not recommended!

CASTLE MENZIES ▶

From the 14th century the lands around Weem were part of the extensive possessions of the chiefs of Clan Menzies and it was here in 1488 that following the destruction by fire of the Menzies stronghold, Comrie Castle. (The ruins of a later replacement of which are 4 miles west of Weem), Sir Robert Menzies built a new mansion, the "Place of Weem."

MOOT HILL ▶

Moot Hill is thought to have been a Hill of Judgement in the Middle Ages. This means that anyone found guilty of a serious crime would be sentenced there after having been tried in the Courthall of Mugdock Castle

SCOTLAND

BLAIR CASTLE ◀

This magnificent castle has been a magnet for visitors for generations—one or two of whom have been turned away with a bucket of boiling oil or a volley of musket fire, but most have been warmly welcomed. Especially these days! Blair was one of the first private houses in Scotland to be opened to the public.

DRUMMOND CASTLE GARDENS ◀

The castle gardens were first laid out in the early 17th century and re-designed and terraced in the early 19th century. However, the gardens you see today were replanted during the 1950's, but a number of important features such as the ancient yew tree hedges and the copper beech trees planted by Queen Victoria to commemorate her visit in 1842 were carefully preserved in the latest scheme.

LOCH LEVEN CASTLE ▶

Loch Leven Castle is located on an island towards the western margin of the loch and it is most famous as the prison of Mary, Queen of Scots, (1542-87) between the summer of 1567, following her surrender at Carberry Hill to her half-brother James Douglas, the 4th Earl of Morton, and the spring of 1568, when she escaped.

DUNKELD CATHEDRAL ◀

No one who knows Dunkeld would wish to dispute that it is one of Scotland's most delightful small towns. It has the great natural advantage of a magnificent setting on the banks of the River Tay.

AUCHTERARDER ▶

The mile and a half long High Street of Auchterarder gave the town its popular name of the "Lang Toon." Golf is synonymous with Auchterarder as this town is the home of Gleneagles, one of the most famous hotels in the world. The town was also the centre of the Perthshire weaving industry.

KENMORE ▲

The village stands at efflux of the River Tay from Loch Tay, six miles west-south-west of Aberfeldy. Kenmore is a neat small place, with picturesque environs—described in famous lines by the poet Robert Burns.

LOCH TURRET ◀

In 1787 on a visit to nearby Crieff, Burns wrote a poem to Euphemia Murray of Auchtertyre and another while hunting wildfowl on Loch Turret.

GLAMIS CASTLE ◀

The earliest records reveal that Glamis Castle was originally a royal hunting lodge owned by the Scottish Crown. The structure then would have been very different from the castle of today. Like most castles, the story of Glamis has been one of additions, alterations and reconstructions to satisfy the needs and aspirations of its owners and the architectural fashions of the day. Glamis Castle was the childhood home of Queen Elizabeth the Queen Mother whose ancestral home it was.

Peter Pan ▲

In this two-storeyed house J. M. Barrie (1860-1937) was born. The upper floors are furnished as they may have been when Barrie lived there. The adjacent house, No 11, houses an exhibition—The Genius of JM Barrie—about Barrie's literary and theatrical works.

Barry Mill ◥

Records show that a mill has occupied the site since at least 1539. The present building was rebuilt in 1814 following a fire. Barry Mill was the last water-powered meal mill to work in Angus, producing oatmeal until the late 1970s and animal feed until 1982. The building is now used to demonstrate the art of milling for visitors.

Royal Palace of Falkland ▶

The Royal Palace of Falkland was the country residence of the Stuart kings and queens when they hunted deer and wild boar in the Fife forest. Mary, Queen of Scots spent some of the happiest days of her tragic life "playing the country girl in the woods and parks." The Palace was built between 1501 and 1541 by kings James IV and James V of Scotland, replacing earlier castle and palace buildings dating from the 12th century, traces of which can still be seen in the grounds.

THE HERMITAGE ◀

The Hermitage sits in 33 acres of mixed conifer and deciduous woodlands that also contains one of Britain's tallest Douglas fir trees as well as the increasingly rare red squirrel. The Hermitage sits above a waterfall and besides the enchanting bridge under which rush the dark waters of the River Braan.

TARVIT MANSIONHOUSE ▼

The present house was virtually rebuilt in 1906 by Sir Robert Lorimer for Mr F. B. Sharp to form a suitable setting for his notable collection of furniture that includes French, Chippendale-style, and vernacular furniture. In addition there are Dutch paintings and pictures by Raeburn and Ramsay, Flemish tapestries, and Chinese porcelain and bronzes.

CRAIL HARBOR ▶

Crail, in The Kingdom of Fife, is a very popular East Neuk village adored by both artists and photographers. Crail harbor is surrounded with little white walled houses with crowstepped gables and red pantile roofs.

HILLS AND LOCH TAY ▲

Crannogs were used as defensive dwellings from as early as the Neolithic Age (5,000 years ago) to as late as the 17th century in some places. They were built by driving timber piles into shallow parts of the lochbed, which then became the supporting frame for the round house itself.

TAY RIVER ▶

The mighty River Tay begins 100 yards west of the village of Kenmore as it flows out of Loch Tay.

SCOTLAND

Aberdeen has many labels that help to give an idea of its style: The Granite City, The Flower of Scotland, The Silver City by the Golden Sands, all names that it wears pride.

Aberdeen is a prosperous cosmopolitan city with a historical old town whose granite stones make the buildings sparkle after rain. Furthermore, Aberdeen has one of Scotland's most striking skylines. The massive granite buildings such as Marishal College, His Majesty's Theatre, and St. Machar's Cathedral, give the city its distinctive look, while historical Old Aberdeen and the fishing village of Footdee, have an incredible air of time gone by.

Some things don't change. You cannot escape the sea here, not since it was founded as a Royal burgh back in 1124. The

influence of the harbor is everywhere (as are the gulls!), and the harvest of the North Sea continues. Where once streamlined clipper ships left the slipways for the China tea trade, now oil executives from all over the world drive to their comfortable homes in the suburbs after working with the prosperous North Sea oil rig industry.

Out in the lands beyond the city the work of rose breeders fills fields and hillsides, and their produce lines roads, streets, parks, gardens, and estates. If you're interested in rose gardens don't miss Crathes Castle, Drum Castle, or Hazlehead Park, Aberdeen. For rock gardens try Leith Hall, Kildrummy, and Ballindalloch Castle, and if alpines are your interest, then make sure that Kildrummy Castle Gardens and Johnston Gardens, Aberdeen, are on your list. For topiary, visit Grant Park, Forres.

ABERDEEN HARBOR ▲
Aberdeen first rose to prominence as a prosperous fishing port for the once abundant North Sea, North Atlantic, and Arctic Ocean fisheries. Now the city is an important centre for North Sea Oil.

PASS OF KILLIECRANKIE ▶
During the Jacobite uprisings there was a battle in Killiecrankie in 1689 when Highlanders defeated a much larger government force under Hugh MacKay. However, the Jacobite leader, Viscount Dundee, was killed. This defeat led to a new road being built through the Pass by General Wade in 1728, so that government inspectors and troops could easily reach the lawless Highlanders.

ABERDEEN AND GRAMPIAN

PITMEDDEN ▲

The centrepiece of this property is the Great Garden, originally laid out in 1675 by Sir Alexander Seton, 1st Baronet of Pitmedden. The garden was restored in the 1950s when the elaborate floral designs were recreated under the guidance of the late Dr James Richardson. Three of the formal parterres were taken from designs possibly used in the gardens at the Palace of Holyroodhouse, Edinburgh in 1647. The fourth parterre is a heraldic design based on Sir Alexander's coat-of-arms.

CASTLE FRASER ◀

The most elaborate Z-plan castle in Scotland, and one of the grandest Castles of Mar, was begun in 1575 by the sixth laird, Michael Fraser, and incorporates an earlier building. The castle was completed in 1636 and was the masterpiece of two great families of master masons, Bell and Leiper. The armorial panel high on the north side of the castle is signed "I Bel." Castle Fraser belongs to the same period of native architectural achievements as two neighbouring castles, Crathes and Craigievar, both owned by the National Trust of Scotland.

ISLE OF SKYE ◀

To the ancient Celts, looking down from the hills, the Isle of Skye was *An t'Eilean Sgitheanach*, the Winged Isle. To the Vikings approaching from the sea, she was *Skuyo* (Sky-a), the Cloud Island.

INVERNESS CASTLE ▶

A castle was built here by Macbeth, which was destroyed by Malcolm Canmore in 1057. It sits on a low cliff on the east bank overlooking the river.

CAIRNGORMS ▼

The granite Cairngorms are a vast high mountain range divided into three blocks by two major passes, Lairig an Laoigh and Lairig Ghru.

SCOTLAND

CAWDOR CASTLE ▶

Built in 1370 around an earlier military structure, Cawdor Castle is famous for being Shakespeare's setting for Duncan's murder by Macbeth in "the Scottish play."

MACLEOD'S TABLE ▼

This is a flat-topped mountain, and it is said that when the clan chief particularly wanted to impress a visitor he held a banquet on the mountain top, surrounded by clansmen carrying torches. At 1,535ft high, this must have made for a chilly entertainment!

EILEAN DONAN CASTLE ▲
Although the island of Eilean Donan has been a fortified site for at least 800 years, the present building largely dates from the early 20th century. Today's castle, which rose from the ruins of its predecessor, was re-built between 1912–32 by Lt Col John MacRae-Gilstrap.

DUNVEGAN CASTLE ▶
Stronghold of the Chiefs of MacLeod for 800 years. Built on a rock once surrounded entirely by salt water, it is unique in Scotland as the only house of such antiquity to have retained its family and roof through the centuries.

SCOTLAND

DUNROBIN CASTLE ◀

Dunrobin is the most northerly of the great houses of Scotland. It is a private house, seat of the Earls and Dukes of Sutherland, and owned by the Countess of Sutherland.

AUTUMN AT LOCH NESS ▼

Loch Ness is of considerable intrinsic scientific interest as Britain's greatest volume of freshwater. However, it is famous on account of the popular but reticent Loch Ness monster that every visitor to Scotland hopes to see.

FIVE SISTERS OF KINTAIL ▶

The Five Sisters of Kintail are a range of peaks connected by a fairly narrow ridge on the north and west sides of Glen Shiel, at their western end. The highest Sister, Sgurr Fhuaran, rises to 3,504ft from the valley floor in one continuous climb.

BEN LOMOND ▼

Ben Lomond is, cloud permitting, a superb viewpoint with views extending across much of the Southern Highlands. Its prominence also probably gave rise to its name; which translates as "Beacon Hill."

SCOTLAND

DUNCANSBY HEAD ◄

The cliffs provide huge numbers of seabirds with safe ledges and shelter from the elements for their chicks .

GLENFINNAN MONUMENT ►

The Glenfinnan Monument was erected in 1815 by Alexander Macdonald of Glenaladale as a tribute to the various clansmen who died fighting for the cause of Prince Charles Edward Stuart.

SANGO SANDS ▼ ◄

Balnakeil and Sangomore are the most accessible beaches, with Sangobeg and Ceannabeinne further to the east. The peninsula is called Faraid Head and is a good observation point for watching puffins and other seabirds.

BLACK MOUNT ▶

The Black Mount is the collective name of the group of hills which form the backdrop for the wild and desolate expanse of Rannoch Moor.

BUACHAILLE ETIVE MOR ▼

Known as the guardian of Glencoe, the Buachaille rises abruptly and in isolation out of the northwest corner of Rannoch Moor. It is probably the most popular mountain in Scotland for climbers. The highest peak is Stob Dearg at 3,353ft.

Quiraing, Skye ◀

The fantastic pinnacles of the Storr and the Quiraing are one of the natural wonders of Scotland.

Loch Clair, Glen Torridon ▲

The loch lies just off the A896 to the east of Glen Torridon. From Loch Clair there is a splendid view of Beinn Eighe, the easternmost of the Torridonian mountains.

Invermoriston ▼

Only eight miles along the shore of Loch Ness, the village of Invermoriston is also steeped in Jacobite romance, like the legendary Seven Men of Moriston and rebel hero Roderick MacKenzie.

THE NESS ▲

The Ness is a river of only six miles in length, draining the renowned loch of the same name as well as a vast hinterland of Highland territory.

RUTHVEN BARRACKS ▼

Built by General Wade as part of the infrastructure put in place by government after the 1715 uprising to control the rebellious Scots.

SCOTLAND

SKYE BRIDGE ◀

The car ferry making the five minute
journey between Kyleakin and Kyle of
Lochalsh was finally made redundant in
1995 with the opening of the contro-
versial Skye Bridge. The whole island is
an area of stunning natural beauty, little
changed since King Haakon anchored
his Norwegian longships there in 1263.

WADES BRIDGE ▶

Colonel Wade founded the Black Watch
and a memorial to the regiment stands
on the river side.

CALEDONIAN CANAL ▼

Stretching from Inverness to Fort
William the majestic Caledonian Canal
is 60 miles long, of which 22 miles is
man made.

SCOTLAND

ISLE OF LEWIS ◄

Lewis is the largest island of the Outer Hebrides. Across the central peat moorland there are hundreds of shallow lochs, so much so that the name Lewis derives from *leogach* meaning "marshy."

ESHA NESS, SHETLAND ►

The red, basalt lava cliffs of Esha ness, in the north-west of Mainland, form some of the most impressive coastal scenery in Shetland. There are over 100 islands in the Shetland group varying in size from a few square yards to hundreds of square miles. Only 14 of the islands are inhabited, of which Mainland is by far the biggest and most populous.

HARRIS AT SUNSET ◄

The island of Harris is separated from Lewis by Loch Seaforth and Loch Resort and six mile barrier of wild moorland and mountain. North Harris is separated from South Harris by the narrow neck of land at Tarbert, the largest village on the island. Harris is primarily composed of tough gneiss rocks which have a bare covering of peat. Islanders are traditionally crofters and fishermen and this is where the famously tough Harris tweed cloth comes from.

JARLSHOF, SHETLAND ▲

Over three acres of prehistoric and Norse remains, spanning 3,000 years from the Stone Age. Here lie oval shaped Bronze Age houses, Iron Age broch and wheel houses, Viking long houses, and medieval farmhouses.

MOUSA BROCH, MOUSA ▶

The finest surviving Iron Age Broch Tower, still over 40 feet high. The work of Prehistoric man, it is a circular tower enclosing a central courtyard.

MUNESS CASTLE, UNST ◀

A fine castelled mansion built in 1600 by Patrick Stewart, Earl of Orkney, who was notorious for his cruelty. Unst is the most northerly place in Britain and is 12 miles long by six miles wide. Its small population is augmented by large numbers of native Shetland ponies.

RONAS HILL, SHETLAND ▶

Joined to the Mainland by the narrow isthmus of Mavis Grind, north Mainland is a vast and magical landscape dominated by Shetland's highest summit, Ronas Hill, 1,486ft high. From the top of the hill on a clear day the whole of Shetland and a long way beyond can be admired.

SPIGGIE BEACH ▶

Shetland's most easterly outpost, with its dramatic and varied coastline provides a wealth of walking opportunities, encompassing beautiful scenery with rugged cliffs, arches, blow-holes, steep geos, stacks, long voes, and beaches with fascinating layers of smooth pebbles.

UNST ▶

The most northerly island in Shetland is also one of the most varied and spectacular, with ultramarine sea, beautiful sun-bleached beaches of pure sand, majestic cliffs and hills, outstanding flora and fauna and national nature reserves of international significance. Beyond the northern tip of Unst is Muckle Flugga —the end of Britain.

SCOTLAND

THE BUTT OF LEWIS ◀

The Butt of Lewis Lighthouse was designed by David Stevenson, Engineer to the Northern Lighthouse Board and a grandfather of the Scottish author Robert Louis Stevenson, famous for writing classics such as *Treasure Island*, *Kidnapped* and *The Strange Case of Doctor Jekyll and Mr Hyde*.

LOCH EYNORT ◀

Tusdale is a lovely glen on the west coast of Skye, a few miles north of Glen Brittle and the Cuillins mountains. At the head of the loch lies the small village of Eynort at the edge of a sheltered beach.

KISMUL CASTLE ▼

The fortress of the Macneil clan, still stands on its own off the island of Barra and Macneil of Macneil (the clan chief) spends most of the year on the island.

LEWIS ▶

Lewis is the largest of the Islands of the Outer Hebrides. The island has many superb beaches on the west side with sweeping sandy coves, many of which are well sheltered from the elements.

BARRA ▼

In 1427 the lands of Barra and South Uist were granted to the chief of Clan MacNeil. The castle of Kisimul was to house and safeguard the clan chiefs for three more centuries. Its proud achievement is that in all its long history the castle was never lost to an enemy.

NORTHERN IRELAND

NORTHERN IRELAND

The cityscape reveals Belfast's shipbuilding heritage with the cranes towering over the waters of the River Lagan. Badly bombed during the Blitz, a modern city has emerged to replace many of the old buildings.

RIVER LAGAN ▶
The river lies at the heart of Belfast's prosperity and has been as busy port for centuries.

At the heart of Northern Ireland lies unspoilt naturalness, which encompasses a beautiful landscape, quality local produce where people are spontaneous in their humour, genuine, hospitable, and welcoming.

To the north is the dramatic coastline of the Causeway Coast and Glens, with its many myths and legends. The Causeway and the Causeway coast have been granted World Heritage status for their unique splendour.

West lies Derry/Londonderry, the capital of creative energy with its poets, storytellers, festivals, and music. Crossing the Sperrins brings you to Belfast city and its surrounding hills.

In the south east lie the Kingdoms of Down where you can enjoy the Mountains of Mourne, Strangford Lough, small fishing villages, wonderful gardens, and historic houses. To the south west, Fermanagh Lakeland offers an inviting haven to refresh and amuse, surrounded by wonderful lakes.

Unless you approach Belfast from the sea you cannot help but come upon the

city suddenly because of its fine setting. Belfast was a village in the 17th century, but now contains nearly half a million people—a third of Northern Ireland's population. Belfast was the engine-room that drove the whirring wheels of the Industrial Revolution in Ulster. The development of industries like linen, rope-making, and shipbuilding doubled the size of Belfast every ten years. The world's largest dry dock is here and the shipyard's giant cranes tower over the port. The doomed RMS *Titanic* was built here in the Harland & Wolff shipyards, as were her sister ships.

In County Antrim the marine drive north from Larne and then west past the Giant's Causeway to the resort of Portrush, follows 60 miles of the most beautiful coast you could imagine. The first 28 miles were blasted out from the chalky cliffs in 1834. When the road was opened to Ballycastle, all nine glens suddenly became accessible and the farmers could at last get to market easily.

As you turn Ulster's top right-hand corner, the green crescent of Murlough Bay comes into sight before the climb to the eerie tableland of Fair Head, and a bird's eye view of Rathlin Island.

"The Mountains o' Mourne sweep down to the sea"—at Newcastle. The sea itself invades the land, forming the great bird sanctuary and yachting paradise of Strangford Lough. St. Patrick sailed into the lough in 432AD and eventually died at Downpatrick.

Armagh has been the spiritual capital of Ireland for over 1,500 years and is the seat of both Protestant and Catholic archbishops. St. Patrick called Armagh "my sweet hill" and built his stone church on the hill where the Anglican cathedral now stands.

Often to be seen is hurley which looks like (and possibly is) the worlds most dangerous game. The sticks are whirled around the players' heads like wooden battle-axes and the ball flies from end to end of the field. The great Irish warlord Cuchelain loved playing this game and it's a great spectator sport.

In Tyrone, apart from Omagh, the county town, Cookstown (justly famous for its sausages) and Dungannon the landscape is almost empty of men but rich in prehistoric and Celtic remains. About one thousand standing stones are a testament to the Stone Age people who passed this way. Well known sites include the Beaghmore stone circles near Cookstown which were uncovered only 40 years ago, and the chambered cairn of Knockmany at the top of a steep wooded hill north of Clogher.

The rivers and lakes of Fermanagh are heavy with fish and Lough Erne has claimed many world coarse angling match records. The trout and salmon fishing is good too that the whole region is a true fisherman's' paradise.

Derry is one of the longest continuously inhabited places in Ireland. The earliest historical references date to the sixth century when a monastery was founded here, but for thousands of years before that people had been living in the vicinity. These "prehistoric" peoples left traces of their existence in the various archaeological sites and objects which often come to light in this area.

MALONE HOUSE ▼

An elegant Georgian mansion set in the parkland of Barnett Demense in South Belfast and home of the Higgin Art Gallery.

BELFAST CASTLE ▼

Completed in 1870 despite having exceeded its budget, it was paid for by Lord Ashley, heir to the title Earl of Shaftesbury.

STORMONT ◄

Stormont was built in the early 1900s
in typical Georgian style. Between 1921
and 1972 it served as the Northern
Ireland Parliament. Following the Good
Friday Agreement it is now the home
of the Northern Ireland Assembly. The
interior floorspace totals nearly five
acres and the building stands at the end
of a mile long driveway in 300 acres of
parkland, which are open to the public.

ST ANNES ►

Belfast Cathedral is an imposing
monument to persistence—it was partly
completed and opened 1890—but only
and finished nearly a century later!

BOTANIC GARDENS ▼

An elegant structure of curved glass and
cast iron, The Palm House (1839), was
recently renovated. In the Tropical
Ravine, plants grow in a sunken glen.

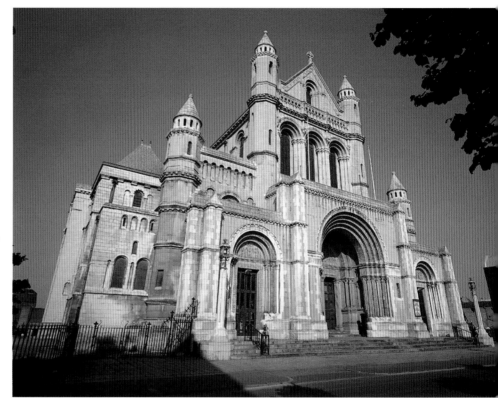

GRAND OPERA HOUSE ▼

The Mennock Pass begins its descent from Wanlockhead and
follows the flow of the Mennock Burn, where visitors can

COUNTY ANTRIM

BALLGALEY ◀

The castle was built in 1625 by James Shaw of Greenock in typical Scottish Baronial style.

CARRICK–A–REDE ◤

The waters around this area of coast are often too rough to be reached by a small boat and it was due to this that local fishermen kept the bridge in order to reach the best places to catch the migrating salmon. The rope bridge is roughly 70ft across and 100ft above the sea. Normally erected in the spring and taken down in the autumn, a salmon bag net is checked and emptied daily between June and August except weekends when it is not fished. The bridge is maintained by the National Trust, a conservation charity.

CARNLOUGH ▼

Winston Churchill inherited the old pub in this charming port at the lower end of Glencloy (which means "valley of the hedges"), one of the nine glens of County Antrim.

DUNLUCE CASTLE ◀
The castle as seen today dates largely from the 16th and 17th centuries when they were built by the MacDonnells, however the outer walls with round towers are attributed to 14th century building by the MacQuillans. The castle can only be reached over a bridge which replaces the original rocky connection. The bridge leads to the "New" Scottish style gatehouse built after the original was destroyed by cannon in 1584 by the Lord Deputy of Ireland, Sir John Perrot.

WHITEROCK BEACH, PORTRUSH ▶
The White Rocks are a famous landmark on the North Coast, the limestone formations containing many fossils from earlier times. The dunes are included in an ongoing conservation program to safeguard their future.

GIANT'S CAUSEWAY ▶
The Causeway proper is a mass of basalt columns packed tightly together. The tops of the columns form stepping stones that lead from the cliff foot and disappear under the sea. Altogether there are 40,000 of these stone columns, mostly hexagonal but some with four, five, seven, and eight sides.

GLENARIFF ◀
The "queen of the glens," with a series of waterfalls plunging down through a gorge traversed by a path crossing rustic bridges. One cascade has the romantic name "tears of the mountain."

IRISH LINEN CENTRE ▶
The Irish Linen Centre and Lisburn Museum houses a major exhibition of the history of Irish linen. It houses an interactive gallery with hands on participation in the linen manufacturing processes, an audio-visual presentation on the lives of workers in a Victorian factory setting, and hand loom weavers producing linen on restored 19th century looms.

MOURNE ◀ AND ▲
The Mourne Mountains are among Ireland's tallest. Slieve Donard, the highest peak, is 2,796ft. There are ten summits over 2,000ft and the range covers some 80 square miles of unspoilt mountain and moorland grandeur.

MOUNTAINS OF MOURNE ▲ ◀
The ridge of mountains gently slope towards the sea into Dundrum Bay. This well forrested area is wonderful for walking through and observing nature. Near the summit of Slieve Croob is the most interesting dolmen in Ireland, the Legananny Tripod-Dolmen.

WARRENPOINT ▲

The town is compact and attractive with neat Victorian terraces and wide streets. Visitors are surprised to learn that this is still one of the busiest ports in Northern Ireland, commercial berthing being out of sight further up the Lough.

MOUNT STUART HOUSE AND GARDENS ◀

The boyhood home of Robert Stewart, Lord Castlereagh. The gardens are among the finest in Europe, with an unrivalled collection of plants, colourful parterres, and vistas.

SILENT VALLEY ▲

The Silent Valley and Ben Crom reservoirs supply thirty million gallons of water a day to Belfast and County Down. All around the dam lies beautiful parklands and wonderful countryside.

LEGANANNY DOLMEN ▶

South of Ballynahinch on the slopes of Slieve Croob (Cratlieve) mountain stands the Legananny Dolmen, one of Ireland's finest Neolithic tombs—country people called them "giants' graves."

GOSFORD PARK ▲
Gosford Forest Park at Markethill, this is the former demesne of Gosford Castle, a mock–Norman battlemented extravaganza. Arboretum, walled garden, nature trail, a camping and caravan site, and Dean Swift's Well and Chair.

THATCHED COTTAGE, MAGHERY ◄
The typical Irish house has changed little over the centuries. Traditionally it is a single story rectangle with a thatched roof of high quality straw or reeds. In the wild and windy westerly regions the thatch is tied to the roof with ropes.

ARMAGH ▶
The name Armagh comes from the Irish *Ard Macha* and means "hill of Macha." Macha is a legendary heroine who was forced to race the King of Ulster's horse even though she was pregnant. After winning but just before she died, she cursed the men of Ulster to suffer the pains of childbirth.

NAVAN CENTRE ◄

Navan Fort, or to give its ancient name, Emain Macha was the spiritual, political, and cultural centre of its day. The legends associated with the site which were first written down in the 7th century, may cast some light on that period. It is tempting to think of Emain in the same light as the Troy of Homer, or the ancient Camelot of King Arthur.

OXFORD ISLAND LOUGH NEAGH ◄

Oxford Island, a National Reserve on the shores of Lough Neagh, offers excellent opportunities for people to get close to nature. It is a peninsula today but was an island prior to 1850's before the lough was successively lowered. The reserve consists of 270 acres with five miles of walks and nature trails that are accessible in all seasons of the year.

CRAIGMORE VIADUCT ►

This eighteen-arch viaduct sweeps across the valley of the Camlough river and the National Trust's Derrymore House. This elegant 18th century cottage was built as a country retreat. It is famous for being the place where the Act of Union was drawn up.

NORTHERN IRELAND

There are six counties in Northern Ireland, or Ulster as it is also known. The capital and administrative centre of Northern Ireland is Belfast and the six regional areas are Donegal, Fermanagh, Down, Antrim, Armagh, Tyrone, and Londonderry. They are independent from the rest of Ireland and belong to the United Kingdom by an English act of Parliament in 1920.

Each county has its own particular flavour and differences. The city of

Belfast lies at the mouth of River Lagan where it flows into Belfast Lough. It became a bust port in the 18th and 19th centuries when it developed huge ship-building yards, most notably those of Harland & Wolff, and Short Brothers. The city has many attractions including fine buildings, ornate churches, museums, the botanic gardens, and Queen's University.

County Down lies east of Belfast and borders the Irish Sea. The Mountains of

COUNTY TYRONE ▲

Near Strabane, is the ancestral home of Woodrow Wilson, 28th president of the United States. The farm is still occupied by the Wilson family, who will show callers round the house.

Mourne are its premier attraction and slope gently towards the Irish Sea. In Downpatrick Cathedral are reputed to lie the remains of St. Patrick.

County Donegal is the least known although it has the longest and most

spectacular coastlines coupled with fantastic beaches. Founded by the Vikings the town of Donegal lies deep in the heart of Donegal Bay at the mouth of the River Eske. County Antrim adjoins the north east coast of the Irish Sea. It is famous for its nine glens that until the 19th century were isolated from each other. Now visitors as well as locals can enjoy the splendours that this unspoilt natural habitat offers. However it is the Giant's Causeway that makes Antrim

unique. This spectacular basalt outcrop was formed 60 million years ago and is one of the wonders of the natural world.

Londonderry or Derry was founded in the 6th century and sits on the banks of the River Foyle. It was the last fortified town to be built in Ireland. Further inland lies Armagh, the ecclesiastical capital of Ireland with its two cathedrals. In Fermanagh lies the Lake District and like Tyrone the county is landlocked and rural in character.

COUNTY TYRONE ▲

On the horizon lie the windswept moors of County Tyrone. Apart from Omagh, the county town, Cookstown (famous for its sausages) and Dungannon, the landscape is almost empty of men but rich in prehistoric and Celtic remains. About one thousand standing stones are a testament to the Stone Age people who passed this way.

ARDBOE CROSS ◀

Ardboe Cross is a national monument which dates from the 10th century and is believed to be the first high cross in Ulster. It stands 18½ feet high with arms of 3½ feet wide. Its 22 panels depict various biblical scenes; Old Testament scenes on east side, and New Testament depictions on the west.

WILSON ANCESTRAL HOMESTEAD ▼

This authentic cottage has remained virtually unchanged since James Wilson, the grandfather of U.S. president Woodrow Wilson emigrated to America in 1807. The ambience of bygone days is relived in front of the traditional hearth fire, and in the carefully conserved rooms complete with authentic artefacts.

BEAGHMORE STONE CIRCLES ▶

This is a mysterious complex of seven Bronze Age stone circles and alignments. These megalithic tombs and the mysterious Beaghmore stone circles stood as silent witnesses to the settlements that thrived here six thousand years ago.

ULSTER HISTORY PARK ▼

The Ulster History Park is an open air museum dedicated to the presentation of the history of human settlement in Ireland over the last 10,000 years. Set in 35 acres in the foothills of the Sperrin Mountains, and laid out in chronological order, it contains reconstructions of some of the monuments of the past, from the flimsy huts of the earliest hunter-gatherers to the fortified manorhouse of the 17th century.

LOWER LOUGH ERNE ◀
In County Fermanagh Lower Lough
Erne contains a number of holy islands
on which there are the remains of
ancient religious settlement and
numerous interesting and enigmatic
stone carvings and remains.

FERMANAGH ▼
Ireland is known for its fine fishing and
Lough Erne is renowned for its trout.
Fishermen arrive in spring to go "dap-
ping." This is when they sit for hours in
a small boat casting locally caught
mayflies to attract the fat trout. The
picturesque hills are a haven for flora
and fauna at all times of the year.

NORTHERN IRELAND

ENNISKILLEN CASTLE ◀

Located on the banks of the Erne, the castle was built in 1612. The Castle Keep houses the Museum of the Royal Inniskilling Fusiliers—displays span the history of the Castle and the development of Enniskillen town. The Curved Barracks includes displays on the country's archaeological and historic monuments.

UPPER LOGH ERNE ▼

Upstream from Enniskillen the lough gets shallower and numerous small islands dot the waters. Here too are remnants from former times with ancient tombstones and strange stone carvings.

DEVENISH ISLAND ▶

In the Middle Ages there was a chain of island monasteries in Lough Erne. Devenish, where a 12th-century round tower stands sentinel, was an important port of call. From the tower's high windows the monks could see approaching strangers. In its cool cavities they rang their bells and hid their sacred relics.

MARGARET GALLAGHER'S COTTAGE ▼

If you want to see how Northern Irelanders lived a hundred years ago, Margaret Gallagher still lives the same way as her ancestors did in this thatched cottage at Belcoo.

SHOP ▲
Irish shops and especially pubs, are often painted in bright cheerful colours, perhaps the better to be seen through the winds and rains of winter.

DERRY ◀
Set in a bend of the River Foyle Derry was founded in the 6th century and still has well preserved 17th century city walls. Derry is laid out on a grid system which radiate out from a central square called the Diamond.

GUILDHALL, DERRY ◀

The Neo-Gothic style Guildhall was built in 1912. Its delightful interior is the main civic and cultural centre and the stained glass windows tell the history of Derry. Many concerts, exhibitions and meetings are held here throughout the year.

APPRENTICE BOYS HALL ▶

The hall, built in 1873, is the centre of celebrations held each year to commemorate the Great Siege of 1689. Part of the annual Apprentice Boys parade each August involves the initiation of new members of the organisation here, inside the city walls that were so dearly defended.

DOWNHILL AND MUSSENDEN TEMPLE ▲

Set on a stunning wild headland with fabulous views over Ireland's north coast is the 18th century estate of Downhill. It includes the renowned Mussenden Temple, Mausoleum and palace ruins.

CARLISLE SQUARE SCULPTURE ▶

The statue is situated at the cityside end of Craigavon Bridge and was unveiled in July 1992, shows two men reaching out to each other. It represents friendship and reconciliation and is the artistic embodiment of the "hands across the divide" aspiration.

INDEX

CREDITS

THE PUBLISHERS WISH TO THANK THE FOLLOWING FOR ALL THEIR HELP
WITH THIS PUBLICATION, INCLUDING THE USE OF IMAGES AND TEXT.

David Angel	Wales Tourist Board.	Simon Whitehead	Heart of England Tourist Board.
Nicola Nash	North West Tourist Board.	Sharon Cadman	The National Trust Sth Region.
Jennie Harrop	Yorkshire Tourist Board	Carol Stears	Shepway District Council.
Mari Surgenor	Northern Ireland Tourist Board	Sian McGuire	Argyll, Tourist Board.
Alex Gibson	South East England Tourist Board	Glenn Lory	Ayrshire & Arran Tourist Board ,
Rosie Kitchen	West Norfolk Borough Council		*Photography by Alistair G Firth*
Sam Gaskell	Poole Tourism	Fiona M Jack	The Highlands of Scotland TB
Philip Mcshane	Strabane District Council	St Mawes Castle	*Photographer Dawn Runnals*
Kirsty Hay	Edinburgh & Lothians TB		Carrick District Council
Penny Wilkinson	Rutland County Council	Michael Goonan	Scenic Photos
RG Thomas	Stanford Hall	Lyn Mowat	East of England Tourist Board
Lisa Mumford	Borough of Charnwood	Tony Richards	Lakeland Cam
	Painswick Rococo Garden Trust	Amanda Goller	Scottish Borders Tourist Board.
Florence Wallace	Longleat House Wiltshire	Alan Mackensie	Western Isles Tourist Board
	(Image copyright Skyscan / Bob Evans)		
Bonnie Vernon	Penshurst Place & Gardens Kent	Edinburgh Chapter	*Pictures courtesy of Edinburgh &*
Jackie Deacon	Herefordshire Council		*Lothians Tourist Board. Photographs by*
Ben Barden	Cumbria Tourist Board		*Harvey Wood, Douglas Corrance,*
Isla Robertson	The National Trust for Scotland.		*Marius Alexander and Gus Cambell*
Karen Houlahan	Derry Visitor & Convention		

USEFUL WEBSITES

www.westcountrynow.com	*South West England*	www.scot-borders.co.uk	*Scottish Borders Tourist*
www.cornish-riviera.org.uk	*Newquay & The Cornish*		*Board*
	Riviera	www.edinburgh.org	*Edinburgh and Lothians*
www.scenicphotos.com			*Tourist Board*
www.southerntb.co.uk	*Southern Tourist Board*	www.scottish.heartlands.org	*Argyll, the Isles, Loch*
www.southeastengland.uk.com	*The South East England*		*Lomond, Stirling &*
	Tourist Board		*Trossachs Tourist Board.*
www.londontouristboard.com	*London Tourist Board*	www.standrews.com/fife	*Kingdom of Fife Tourist*
www.capital-calling.com	*Londons Tourist Guide*		*Board*
www.eastofenglandtouristboard.com	*East of England*	www.perthshire.co.uk	*Perthshire Tourist Board*
	Tourist Board	www.host.co.uk	*Highlands of Scotland*
www.visitheartofengland.com	*The Heart of England*		*Tourist Board*
	Tourist Board	www.witb.co.uk	*Western Isles Tourist*
www.yorkshirevisitor.com	*Yorkshire Tourist Board*		*Board*
www.visitnorthwest.com	*North West Tourist Board*	www.angusanddundee.co.uk	*Angus & Dundee Tourist*
www.northumbria-tourist-board.org.uk	*Northumbria*		*Board.*
	Tourist Board	www.agtb.org	*Grampian and Aberdeen*
www.golakes.co.uk	*Cumbria Tourist Board*		*Tourist Board*
www.visitwales.com	*Wales Tourist Board*	www.visitorkney.com	*Orkney Tourist Board*
www.visitscotland.com	*Scottish Tourist Board*	www.shetland-tourism.co.uk	*Shetland Islands Tourism*
www.galloway.co.uk	*Dumfries and Galloway*	www.eastofenglandtouristboard.com	*East of England*
	Tourist Board		*Tourist Board*
www.ayrshire-arran.com	*Ayrshire and Arran Tourist*	www.lakelandcam.co.uk	
	Board	www.discovernorthernireland.com	*Nortern Ireland Tourist*
www.seeglasgow.com	*Greater Glasgow & Clyde*		*Board*
	Valley Tourist Board		